The Eucharistic Congress

Dublin 1932

The Eucharistic Congress
Dublin 1932

Rory O'Dwyer

N

First published 2009
Nonsuch Ireland
119 Lower Baggot Street,
Dublin 2
www.nonsuchireland.com

British Library Cataloguing in Publication Data.
A catalogue record for this book is available from the British Library.

ISBN 978 1 84588 950 0

Typesetting and origination by The History Press
Printed and bound in Great Britain by Athenaeum Press Ltd.

Tabula Rerum

Gratiae Agendae

I wish to acknowledge my gratitude to the following for their support and assistance in researching this topic: Noelle and Evelyn at the Dublin Diocesan Archives; staff at the National Archives of Ireland; staff at the National Library of Ireland; staff at the Central Catholic Library; staff at the *Irish Catholic*; Linda Longmore at Veritas House; Melissa and Grace at the Knock Museum; Canon Flaherty at the Pro-Cathedral; Lelia O'Reilly; Tony Behan; Niall Dardis at Dublin Port Archives; Frank and Paul O'Reilly; Frank Fitzgerald; Mary Bennett; Nuala Treanor; Louis Hogan; Ursula Fry; Liam Keogh; Gertrude Madders; Billy Ramsay; Frank O'Brien; Nancy Sharkey; Mary Halley; Kay Downey; Winnie Quinlan; Mary McEvoy; Nuala Murphy; Sonnie McElligott; Mary Hodge; Denis O'Shaughnessy; Gerry McCready; Marius Ó hEarcáin; Rita Kenny; May Hayes; Margaret Boland; Ursula Burns; Kevin O'Connell; Miriam Tighe; Elizabeth Purcell; Benedict Daly; Bridie Godwin; Michael McAleer; Ursula Fry; Maureen Kelly; Fr Eddie Gallagher; Jim Lowney; Kathleen Kirby; Monica Hurson Kelly; Brian Callanan; Kevin Burns, and Sheila Lynch. Maurice Hartigan's research on the Catholic laity of Dublin in the period has been of great value to the author. Special thanks to my willing and intrepid mother, Mary, to my aunt Monica, to my wife, Margot, and daughter, Aoibhe, for their affectionate forbearance.

Praefatio

The 31st International Eucharistic Congress, held in Dublin in 1932, is one of the most remarkable public events to have taken place in Ireland in the twentieth century. The Congress generated a level of enthusiasm among Irish people that has few real parallels. With extremely favourable weather conditions prevailing in the run up to and during the event, the country was in a suitably festive mood and the Congress left an unforgettable impression on all who witnessed it; it was a touchstone in the lives of those who participated. The sheer scale of the event bore striking testimony to the pride in identity, both national and religious, which patently guided the hundreds of thousands of people who participated in the Congress. In this regard it has often been noted how the Congress was one of those events in the early decades of Irish independence which made manifest, in this case very dramatically, the Catholic nature of the new state.

Common perceptions of the Ireland of this time are of a dull and drab society – the word 'joyless' has been applied. However, the Congress emerges from the same period as surely the most colourful, vibrant and joyful mass public celebration in the history of this island. It was an event that elevated people on various levels, providing enrichment both spiritually and psychologically. If it was a temporary escape from very harsh economic realities on another level, particularly for the poor of Dublin (who were specially celebrated by the international media during the Congress), then it was a most welcome escape for all concerned. The Congress deserves close study as it was the greatest religious festival in Irish history but also, more importantly, because it was an event in which a whole culture (one which had an enormous influence on how so many people in Ireland lived their lives) was at its very apex. As Irish society has changed so much since the early 1930s, a study of the Congress can help to reveal much of the Ireland of that bygone and sometimes misunderstood era.

This book is divided into four chapters: outlining the background to the Congress; highlighting the extraordinary reception of the Papal League and many other notable visitors; profiling the various events, and analysing the social and political aspects. It is intended that the appendix, with its combination of important contemporary documentation (including remarkable legislation) along with vivid personal recollections of various participants in the Congress, will help to further inform upon and even recapture something of the tremendous spirit and atmosphere with the Eucharistic Congress created in Dublin in the summer of 1932.

Origo

Although the Congress holds a special place in Irish history, such events, if not on quite as large a scale, had been taking place in various parts of the world since the late nineteenth century. Defined as gatherings of ecclesiastics and laymen 'for the purpose of celebrating and glorifying the Holy Eucharist and of seeking the best means to spread its knowledge and love throughout the world' (*Catholic Encyclopaedia*, 1910), international Eucharistic Congresses, held generally every two years in this period, were major demonstrations of global Catholicism that attracted considerable pageantry and attention. By the early 1930s the Congresses was well established as the premier international religious event of the Catholic world.

The first Congress took place in Lille, in north-east France in 1881, the inspiration of a devout French woman, Marie Tamisier. She had organised public meetings in honour of the Blessed Sacrament which gradually took the form of pilgrimages to shrines sanctified in previous years by Eucharistic miracles. By 1874 the support and enthusiasm aroused gave definite shape to the movement towards the establishment of international Eucharistic Congresses, and in 1878 papal approval was obtained. During the next few years preliminary organisation took place for a Congress in Lille lead by Mlle Tamisier and Monsignor Gaston de Segur, who was appointed President of the Organising Committee. The Congress was a considerable success and great displays of piety were reported. The movement gained in vigour and scope over the following years. In 1893 the Jerusalem Congress marked the unity of Catholics of the East and of the West. This continued to be a feature of the Congresses – later many churchmen of the Eastern (Byzantine/Slavonic) Rite travelled to the Dublin Congress.

The Congresses became increasingly international by the early twentieth century. The first held in the English-speaking world took place in London in 1908. The official visit of a Papal Legate to London was the first since the Reformation. There was a significant Irish participation in this Congress. Even the Archbishop of Westminster Francis Bourne who hosted the Congress (and who would much later travel to the Dublin Congress as a Cardinal) was of a proud Irish background, as indeed were many of the English Catholic hierarchy. This London Congress was, however, marred when it was announced that the Eucharistic procession through the streets of the host city (the supreme function of the Congress) would not take place, at the request of the British Government, following protests from several ultra-Protestant groups. Somewhat similar protests also took place on a smaller scale in Belfast and in London in 1932.

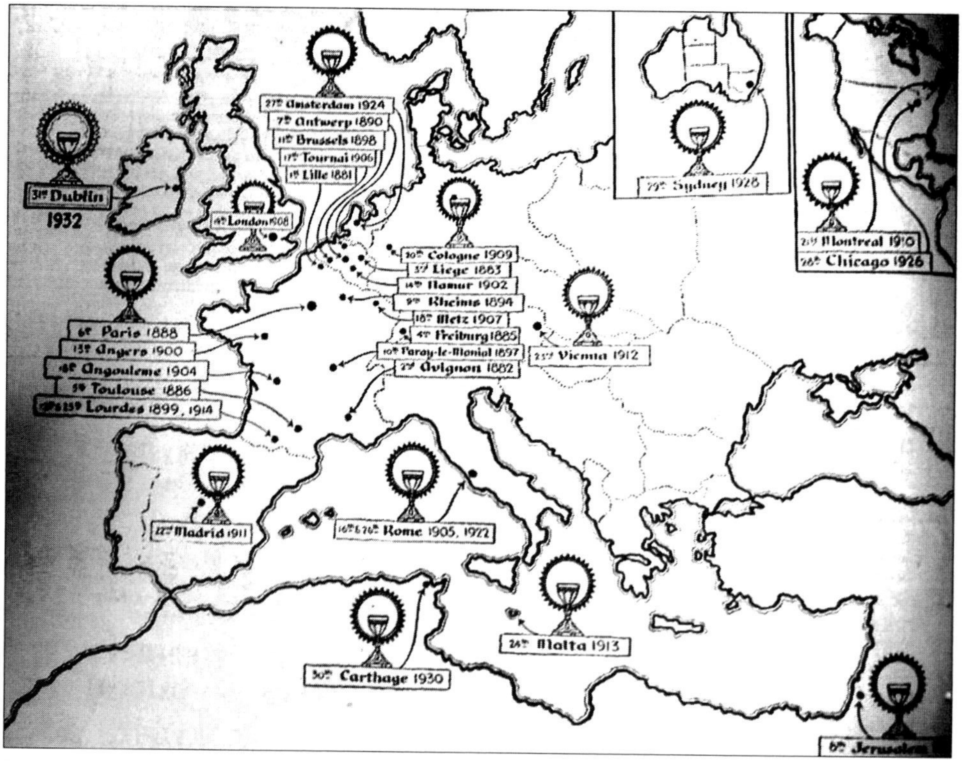

Map featuring the venues for all International Eucharistic Congresses up to 1932. (*Courtesy of Dublin Diocesan Archives, Eucharistic Congress Collection.*)

Previous Congresses

Lille, France, 1881
Avignon, France, 1882
Leige, Belgium, 1883
Fribourg, Switzerland, 1885
Toulouse, France, 1886
Paris, France, 1887
Antwerp, Belgium, 1890
Jerusalem, Palestine, 1893
Rheims, France, 1894
Paray-le-Monial, France, 1897
Brussels, Belgium, 1898
Lourdes, France, 1899
Angers, France, 1901
Namur, Belgium, 1902
Angouleme, France, 1904
Rome, Italy, 1905
Tournai, Belgium, 1906
Metz, Germany, 1907
London, England, 1908
Cologne, Germany, 1909
Montreal, Canada, 1910
Madrid, Spain, 1911
Vienna, Austria, 1912
Malta, 1913
Lourdes, France, 1914
[Suspension of Congresses owing to the First World War]
Rome, Italy, 1922
Amsterdam, Holland, 1924
Chicago, United States, 1926
Sydney, Australia, 1928
Carthage, Africa, 1930

The possibility of a Congress taking place in Ireland was discussed by Irish and Irish-American ecclesiastics attending the 1926 Congress in Chicago. The issue was again raised at a meeting of the bishops of Ireland in October of that year. A proposal was later forwarded to the Permanent Committee of International Eucharistic Congresses in Belgium, which formally announced acceptance of the Irish proposal in December 1929. The Catholic Emancipation Centenary Celebrations held earlier that year in Ireland were to a verifiable extent a pilot or test-case for the staging of a Eucharistic Congress. References were made during those celebrations to a larger event in the near future. It is clear that the Eucharistic Congress was seen as being of greater significance than the commemoration of the Catholic Emancipation Act (properly Catholic Relief Act) of 1829. Whereas the celebrations in 1929 were of a national character, it was obvious those of 1932 would be international and involve extensive contact with clergy and laity from abroad.

The Irish hierarchy had earlier decided that that no church collections would be made for the centenary celebrations in anticipation of a great collection later for the Congress. The programme and nature of the events in 1932 were remarkably similar to those in Dublin in 1929, though on a considerably more massive scale. The emancipation celebrations had taken place over several days, beginning with a solemn votive Mass in the Pro-Cathedral, followed by a large garden party held in the grounds of Blackrock College, public lectures in the Mansion House and elsewhere, a great Mass attended by half a million people in the Phoenix Park, and an impressive procession of the Blessed Sacrament from the Park to Watling Street Bridge towards the city centre. In November 1929 it was announced unofficially from Rome that the 1932 Congress would take place in Dublin. The celebrations in 1929 helped to

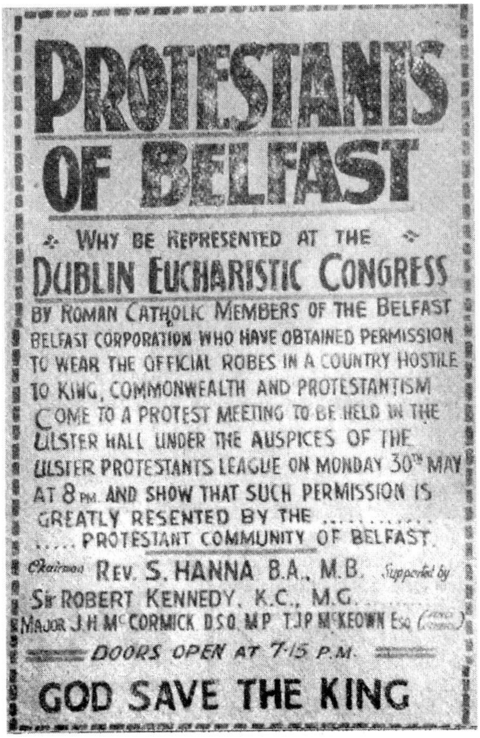

Facsimile of a poster exhibited on Belfast hoardings shortly before the Congress, protesting about Belfast Aldermen (presumably Catholic) travelling to Dublin with their ceremonial robes. The BBC received numerous protests over the broadcasting of the Congress on British Radio. (*Courtesy of Dublin Diocesan Archives, Eucharistic Congress Collection.*)

alleviate concerns as to whether a large-scale event requiring exceptional organisation, co-ordination and mass co-operation, could be carried off in Ireland without the risk of national humiliation. The sense of a psychological importance on a national level (in what was an overwhelmingly Catholic nation) to carry off what was a great international Catholic event, while also challenging a national stereotype, was very evident from the earliest stage.

Whereas the emancipation celebrations were commemorating a political act secured by a remarkable Irish political organisation (the Catholic Association), an international Eucharistic Congress was a mainly spiritual occasion which would increase levels of devotion among the Irish laity. Although Irish Catholicism has been seen as very narrow and insular in this period, Irish Catholics were certainly conscious that they were part of a wider Church, displaying much interest in the fate of Catholics in Spain, Italy, Mexico and Germany. The staging of an international Eucharistic Congress in Dublin could help assign to Ireland its proper place in this wider Catholic world. In 1932 there would be frequent references (made by Irish clergy and Irish commentators) to Irish Catholics as the most steadfast and loyal Catholics in the world. The Congress would see the Catholic nation consciously on show to the world, proudly displaying its religious and national identity. The Congress would also see the most emphatic welcome ever given to large groups of visitors to the country. This was the very opposite of insularity.

Pontifical High Mass in the Phoenix Park during the Catholic Emancipation Centenary Celebrations in 1929. (*Courtesy of the Dublin Diocesan Archives, Eucharistic Congress Collection.*)

The Procession of the Blessed Sacrament during the Catholic Emancipation Centenary Celebrations in 1929. (*Courtesy of the Dublin Diocesan Archives, Eucharistic Congress Collection.*)

Over two and a half years before the Eucharistic Congress took place in Dublin plans were already being conceived for a vast Congress which would be larger than any held up to that point. Given the small size of Ireland, the general material impoverishment of Irish society and the comparatively tiny population, it was a strikingly audacious vision. In January 1930, just weeks after the official acceptance of the Irish proposal to stage a Congress, a Secretary to the Congress, Fr David Molony, was appointed by the Archbishop of Dublin, Edward Byrne, the official sponsor of the Congress. Frank O'Reilly, Executive Secretary of the Catholic Truth Society of Ireland, was appointed Director of Organisation of the Congress. O'Reilly was a proponent of the Catholic action movement of the period (promoting Catholic influence in Ireland) and had already displayed his organisational flair during the emancipation centenary celebrations in 1929 as the key member of the organisation committee. He was fortunate in that he could call up many of those who had been involved in organising the 1929 celebrations. In his planning for the Eucharistic Congress O'Reilly would reveal himself to be a man of very considerable organisational genius.

Although a supreme governing committee was established (consisting of all of the archbishops and bishops in Ireland), on a practical level it was O'Reilly who co-ordinated virtually everything, in Dublin at least. In the immediate wake of the Congress, journalists

Benediction on Watling Street Bridge during the Catholic Emancipation Centenary Celebrations in 1929. (*Courtesy of the Dublin Diocesan Archives, Eucharistic Congress Collection.*)

The President of the Permanent Committee of Eucharistic Congresses, Mgr Heylen, Bishop of Namur. (*Courtesy of Dublin Diocesan Archives, Eucharistic Congress Collection.*)

Edward Byrne, Archbishop of Dublin (1921–1940), the sponsor of the Eucharistic Congress. (*Courtesy of Dublin Diocesan Archives, Eucharistic Congress Collection.*)

who interviewed him were particularly struck by his encyclopaedic knowledge of every detail regarding the Congress. He co-ordinated with great dedication the various committees – the National Eucharistic Congress League (responsible for the spiritual preparations around the country), the General Executive Committee (responsible for the preparations in Dublin), and the Executive Committee (providing frequent liaison with the archbishop of Dublin) – along with a whole series of sub-committees set up to carry out the myriad details of preparation necessary for the Congress: Accommodation Sub-Committee; Catering Sub-Committee; Decorations Sub-Committee; Traffic Sub-Committee; Ceremonial Sub-Committee; Music Sub-Committee; City Decorations Sub-Committee; Medical Sub-Committee; Stewarding Sub-Committee; Reception Sub-Committee; Transport Sub-Committee; Volunteer Motor-Transport Sub-Committee; Literary Sub-Committee; Housing Sub-Committee, and Camp Sub-Committee. All of these sub-committees met regularly from 1930 and O'Reilly appears to have attended every meeting. As the voluminous minutes of these meetings clearly indicate, he was a bright, practical, highly informed and lively participant in all discussions.

***

Above: The National Eucharistic Congress League, with representatives from every diocese of Ireland, organised the spiritual preparations around the country. The Archbishop of Cashel, Revd J.M. Harty (front row, fifth from left) was Chairman. Note Frank O'Reilly (back row, far right). (*O'Reilly Collection*.)

Left: Frank O'Reilly, Director of Organisation. (*O'Reilly Collection*.)

Frank O'Reilly

Frank O'Reilly was born in Drogheda in 1884 and educated by the Christian Brothers in Drogheda and Belfast. Between 1904 and 1918 he was an official in the surveyor's department of the Post Office. He first displayed his gifts for planning and organisation during the 1913 Lockout when he helped to distribute food to strikers' children. In 1918 he was appointed as secretary of the Catholic Truth Society of Ireland (CTSI) and instigated a necessary reorganisation of the society. Following his very prominent role in organising the 1929 celebrations, O'Reilly became the first member of the laity ever to be appointed director of organisation of an international Eucharistic Congress. Shortly after the Congress he was conferred a Knight Commander of the Order of St Gregory and received an honorary doctorate from the National University of Ireland, along with various other distinctions in recognition of his exceptional achievement in 1932. He continued to work with the CTSI (returning to relative obscurity) until his retirement in 1950. He died in 1957.

***

Although it is frequently implied that the Irish Government organised the Congress, this simply was not the case in large part. It was, however, obviously extremely important to have the support of the Government. In that respect it was never likely that O'Reilly and his colleagues would have difficulty, as a precedent had been set in 1929, but it should be noted that neither the Cumann na nGaedheal Government in power for most of the preparatory phase of the Congress or indeed the Fianna Fáil minority Government in power in the immediate run up to and during the Congress events, revealed themselves to be particularly generous financially towards the Congress.

Shortly after being appointed Director of Organisation, O'Reilly sought a meeting with President W.T. Cosgrave. The meeting took place in February 1930 and O'Reilly placed a long list of requests before the president:

(i) Use of military barracks for housing visitors, e.g.:
  (a) Royal Hospital, Kilmainham.
  (b) Hibernian Military School.
  (c) Any other barracks which might be available.
(ii) Loan of spare beds and bedding.
(iii) Closing of National Schools.
(iv) Loan of National Schools for hostels.
(v) Suggested message from President asking all persons, without reference to creed or class, to provide accommodation.
(vi) Camping places – accommodation in the Curragh Camp; use of military fields for camping or parking of motor cars.
(vii) Parking for aeroplanes.
(viii) Salute of guns at consecration.
(ix) Salute of guns at benediction.
(x) Post Office – cancellation stamp; special stamp to commemorate occasion;

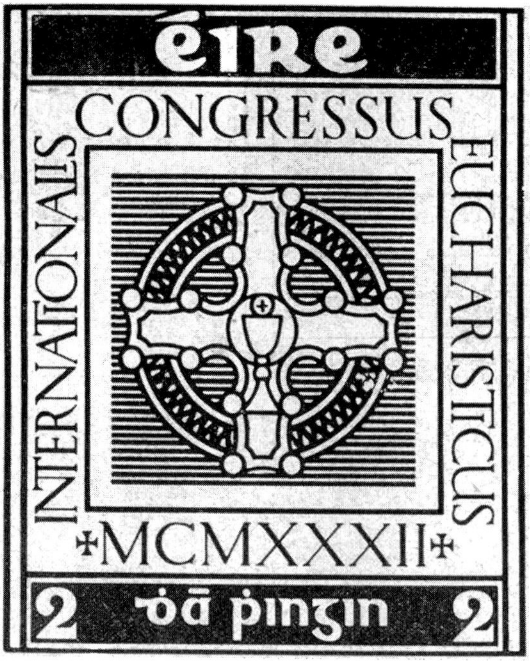

The Eucharistic Congress Stamp designed by G. Atkinson first appeared in May 1932. The design features a chalice set against the Cross of Cong, almost identical to the Congress crest. (*Courtesy of Dublin Diocesan Archives, Eucharistic Congress Collection.*)

broadcasting.

(xi) Message for success of the Congress.

(xii) Reception of Papal Legate.

(xiii) Use of army for route of processions, use of volunteer reserve for stewarding; use of police for stewarding.

These requests were later discussed at a meeting of the executive council where concerns were raised by the notoriously stringent (some would say penurious) and highly cautious Department of Finance, that any spending on the Congress would have to be carefully regulated. An inter-departmental committee on the Congress was established, chaired by J.J. McElligott, the secretary of the Department of Finance and head of the civil service. McElligott quickly issued a circular to all government departments stating that each department 'must refer for priority for expenditure to the department of finance in accordance with the usual procedure' before spending on the Congress. Frank O'Reilly's request for state funding for the amplification system in the Phoenix Park was refused. The stringent approach was perhaps exemplified in a letter from the Department of Posts and Telegraphs to O'Reilly requesting the Congress organisers pay for the dye needed to produce the special Congress stamp. O'Reilly refused to comply with the request.

When O'Reilly met with McElligott in January 1931 it was made very clear that the Government 'were not in a position to undertake expenditure on behalf of the Congress and could only do so after approaching the Oireachtas and securing its consent to the specific appropriation of moneys for that purpose. This the government were not anxious to do.' O'Reilly argued that the state had a role to play in providing accommodation for the large number of visitors expected – this he considered a national concern, and therefore it was reasonable to expect the Government to co-operate with the Congress Committee. McElligott later insisted, however, that other than providing the army for stewarding and ceremonial duties, the furthest the Government could go was in receiving the Papal Legate with full honours on arrival and providing him with a state reception.

The Fianna Fáil Government which came to power in March 1932 displayed somewhat more willingness to approve expenditure on the Congress than the previous Cumann na nGaedheal Government. At a cabinet meeting on 2 April it was decided that, despite the relative expense involved, a cavalry escort with special dress uniform would be provided for the Papal Legate. This was an inspired decision, as the 'Blue Hussars' brought great pomp and ceremony to all occasions they graced. They provided a much appreciated sense of class and were very warmly received by the public. Along with a decision later to charter a special boat and train to convey the Papal Legate to London on his return journey to Rome, the Fianna Fáil Government also decided that the construction of the new broadcasting station in Athlone would be set as a most urgent priority, in order that the Congress could be broadcast throughout Ireland and around much of the world.

The new broadcasting station in Athlone contained a high-powered 60kw transmitter which facilitated the broadcasting of the Congress as far away as Moscow. If work at the station had not proceeded so far ahead of the original schedule the Congress would have been broadcast across Europe from Daventry in England. This would not have fitted very well with the sense of the Congress as a celebration of an independent Irish Catholic identity. The Athlone station was not, however, entirely complete in June 1932. Apparently the building was not properly

A portion of the vast crowd which gathered in Corrigan Park, Belfast, to listen to the broadcast of High Mass in the Phoenix Park, 26 June 1932. Similar gatherings (if not quite as large) to listen to the same broadcast took place in cities, towns and villages throughout Ireland. (*Courtesy of Dublin Diocesan Archives, Eucharistic Congress Collection.*)

Éamon de Valera, President of Executive Council of the Irish Free State during the Eucharistic Congress. (*Courtesy of National Library of Ireland.*)

roofed at the time and there was a serious danger of the new equipment becoming damaged if there was heavy rainfall when the transmitter was in operation. Fortunately the weather was exceptionally good during the Congress period, with only a few very light showers (seldom remembered). The broadcasting station was officially opened on 6 February 1933. In his speech at the official launch of the building the President, Éamon de Valera, highlighted the importance of the close connection with the Irish diaspora, something which the Congress had emphatically demonstrated, 'Droichead nua Átha Luain is ea é, droichead idir na Gaeil in Éireann agus Gaeil in imirce.' ('It is the new bridge of Athlone, a bridge between the Irish in Ireland and the emigrant Irish.')

Decorating the Metropolis

The Dublin Congress took place over five days (22–26 June) in a city decorated and beautified to an exceptional degree. All of the great buildings of the city were floodlit and

Miss Susan O'Farrell, a member of the Argentine delegation to the Eucharistic Congress, decorating the Lord Mayor of Dublin, Alfie Byrne, with the delegation's badges, June 1932. (*Courtesy of Dublin Diocesan Archives, Eucharistic Congress Collection.*)

usually bedecked with flowers and shrubs. The City Decorations Committee had been offering advice and supplying information to residents of Dublin regarding decorations long in advance of the event. Visiting journalists and commentators, including the well-known Catholic intellectual G.K. Chesterton, were struck by the efforts of Dublin people, most especially the impoverished tenement dwellers, to embellish their native streets and laneways with bunting, festoons, banners, garlands, floral arrangements (including the omnipotent window-box in full flower), grottos, shrines and various other forms of religious decoration. Chesterton, who later published *Christendom in Dublin*, reflecting on his experiences at the Congress, revelled in the truly democratic support for the event. Journalists noted how visitors were often so struck by the piety of groups of locals in tenement Dublin gathering to pray around a crudely arranged shrine, that they felt instinctively compelled to join in themselves.

***

A shrine in tenement Dublin, June 1932. Notice how well dressed the children are in this picture, despite the fact that they are probably from the tenements and living in poverty. (*Courtesy of National Library of Ireland.*)

Decoration schemes for Dublin Statues for the Congress

O'Connell Statue: Bambusa, cupressus (in variety), dracaena, polyantha roses, phormias, lobelia singles, thuya, Paul Scarlet geraniums, shrubs, including golden macro, grise lines, senecios, veronicas, olaria as phromiums.

Grattan statue: Standard bays, retinospora, golden shrubs, cupressus lawsonia, hydrangeas, phormias, maguerites, large bamboos, alumii, dordy-linos, geraniums.

Moore Statue: Standard tubbed bays, phormiums, golden shrubs, veronicas, dwarf shrubs, veronicas, roses, bambusa, cryptomoria, cordylines, retinospora, cupressus, hydrangeas.

O'Brien Statue: Golden retinospora, golden cupressus, veronicas, geraniums (in variety), cordylines, alumii, bambusa, roses.

The statues of Parnell, Sir John Gray, Father Mathew and the new statue of the Sacred Heart were also decorated. Nelson's Pillar was also profusely decorated as flower-sellers arranged very attractive displays at the base.

Decorations at Bank of Ireland, College Green. The great buildings of the city were all decorated and floodlit at night. (*Courtesy of Dublin Diocesan Archives, Eucharistic Congress Collection.*)

These decorations on Dominick Street would have been paid for by the residents of the tenement houses. Many families endured privation to ensure their dwellings were decorated to their satisfaction. (*Courtesy of Dublin Diocesan Archives, Eucharistic Congress Collection.*)

Shrine and decoration on a house on Parnell Road, Harold's Cross. (*Courtesy of Dublin Diocesan Archives, Eucharistic Congress Collection.*)

Typical window decoration with flowers, candles and statue of Christ the King. The candles (lit every night) were encouraged by the clergy as a symbol of welcome to foreign pilgrims and emigrant Irish returning to Ireland for the Congress. Many would have also cultivated their own window boxes. Leaflets were distributed by the Congress Decorations Committee with advice on the making and cultivation of window boxes. (*Courtesy of Dublin Diocesan Archives, Eucharistic Congress Collection.*)

The Daniel O'Connell Statue surrounded by plants and shrubbery. (*Courtesy of Dublin Diocesan Archives, Eucharistic Congress Collection.*)

Official Crest of the 31st International Eucharistic Congress

The crest was described in the official Advance Programme as being:

> Catholic and Irish in conception and execution. It is based on the famous Cross of Cong, a perfect example of Irish ecclesiastical art. The head of the cross, which is a processional one, is reproduced in the design with the staff omitted. The beautiful Celtic interlacing in the panels is copied from the original. The chalice embodied in the design is not a representation of any actual chalice, but rather an approximation to one such as would be made by a contemporary Irish Craftsman working in the Celtic tradition. The Host is designed in the universal mode of Eucharistic symbolism. The Latin inscription 'International Eucharistic Congress at Dublin' is in Celtic script, after the manner of the Irish artist-scribes.

The Congress badge was available as a broach, pendant or stud. The adult badge (with gold gilt and blue enamel) cost 1*s*. The children's badge, which was smaller and did not have the gold gilt, cost 4*d*. As is evident in so many photographs of the Congress, the badges were widely worn. They proved a very useful source of funding for the Congress organisers.

***

The following passage is from Chesterton's *Christendom in Dublin* (Sheed & Ward, London, 1932) pp14–16:

> The extraordinary thing was this. I have driven through many such arcades and triumphal arches in many such festive cities. And of nearly all of them it is true to say that any man who strayed from those festive highways would find the festivities fading away. He would find more or fewer flags in this or that side-street; he would not even expect to find so many as there were in the main street. In this one festivity all that common sense was reversed. It was truly like the celestial topsy-turvydom in which the first shall be last. Instead of the main stream of colour flowing down the main streets of commerce, and overflowing into the crooked and neglected slums, it was exactly the other way; it was the slums that were the springs. There were the furnaces of colour; there were the fountains of light; it was as if whatever hidden thing shone here and there in those passionate transparencies was shining in the darkest place; as if the dark heart of the town pumped forth that purple blood, ending in a mere trickle on the highway. I know of no other way of describing it; for I have never seen anything like it in my life.
>
> In that strange town, the poorer were the streets, the richer were the street decorations. They were decorations of a queer kind, as may well be imagined; and yet the decorations were really and truly decorative. They had that triumphant harmony that comes from the complexity of crude colours; for colours always harmonise as long as there are enough of them. That is the secret of much Oriental art; and in that sense these mean streets glowed and glared like Oriental bazaars. But there was something in them that is freshness; or the spirit of something that is born again. I felt in a nameless fashion that I myself was born again; and was passing through

The triumphal arch, with the Congress crest featured over the middle arch, erected at the Parkgate Street entrance to the Phoenix Park. The original gates were removed for the occasion. (*O'Reilly Collection.*)

The crest of the Eucharistic Congress, Dublin 1932. (*Courtesy of Dublin Diocesan Archives, Eucharistic Congress Collection.*)

Above: Congress Badge. (*Courtesy of Dublin Diocesan Archives*.)

Left: G.K. Chesterton.

A grotto in tenement Dublin, June 1932. Over 100,000 people lived in dilapidated tenements in Dublin at this time. Contemporary fears that the city slums might be a breeding ground for communism were proved unfounded; the Congress demonstrated spectacularly the attachment of the city poor to their faith. It also highlighted their remarkable community spirit. (*Courtesy of Dublin Diocesan Archives.*)

'Not Seville, but Dublin' – group gathered to pray at shrine in tenement Dublin. (*Courtesy of Dublin Diocesan Archives, Eucharistic Congress Collection.*)

a sort of supernatural toyshop. All that we feel in infancy about coloured lanterns lit suddenly from within, or peep-shows revealing vividly coloured figures and landscapes, or magic flowers that are made to open by a conjuring trick – all that secret dawn of infancy inhabited those blind alleys and back corners of Dublin. As in a transformation scene, walls might have grown transparent; there were changes in substance and in light. Men who could not paint had painted pictures on their walls; and somehow painted them well. Men who could hardly write had written up inscriptions; and somehow there were dogmas as well as jokes. Somebody wrote 'Long Live St Patrick', as hoping that he might recover from his recent indisposition. Somebody wrote, 'God Bless Christ the King'; and I knew I was staring at one of the great paradoxes of Christianity.

***

As Dublin was chosen as the venue for the Congress – ostensibly at least – to celebrate the 1500th anniversary of the beginning of St Patrick's Christianising mission in Ireland, Early Christian Ireland was often a theme in the decoration. Versions of ecclesiastical artwork associated with that period (such as the beautiful designs found in the Book of Kells) featured prominently in the multifarious material published about the Congress, for which there was a phenomenal demand. 'Celtic' interlace designs were predominant in the Congress ephemera, thus reinforcing the link to ancient Catholic Ireland. The great achievements of the early Church fathers in 'golden age' Ireland were celebrated proudly. A replica Round Tower, for example, was erected at College Green. With the many distinguished prelates from around the globe visiting Dublin for the Congress, along with the international media interest, there was a definite sense that Ireland was on show to the world.

The visual manifestations of enthusiasm for the Congress were matched by the very notable levels of religious observance in advance of and during the event. Thousands participated in retreats and special services to pray for the Congress. Diocesan and parochial units participating in the Congress were organised throughout Ireland by a Eucharistic Congress League which included representatives from every diocese in the country. A 'Crusade of Prayer' was organised for the success of the Congress, involving thousands of people. From the earliest preparations the event was emphasised as a national celebration with every parish in Ireland participating. It is estimated that over 315 million spiritual acts were performed, both in Ireland and in Irish communities around the world, for the success of the Congress. As the event approached there was an almost palpable sense of spiritual energy. A triduum was held in all the churches of the archdiocese of Dublin in the final run up to the Congress.

***

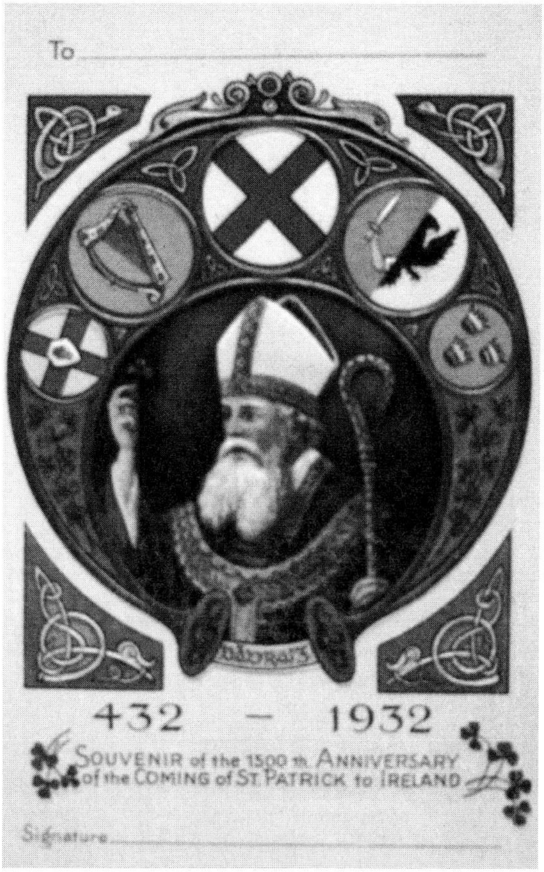

Congress Souvenir Postcard. (*Courtesy of Tony Behan.*)

Record of spiritual acts performed for the success of the Congress

Totals calculated at Archbishop's House in April 1932 (two months before the Congress):

Masses	20,530,251
Holy Communions	14,194,210
Sp. Communions	58,036,613
Benedictions	5,840,019
Holy Hours	6,133,046
Visits to the Blessed Sacrament	40,273,412
Stations of the Cross	11,448,100
Acts of Self-Denial	37,709,110
Alms	905,239
Office of B.V.M.	5,487,171
Other Spiritual Acts	114,903,174
Total	315,460,345

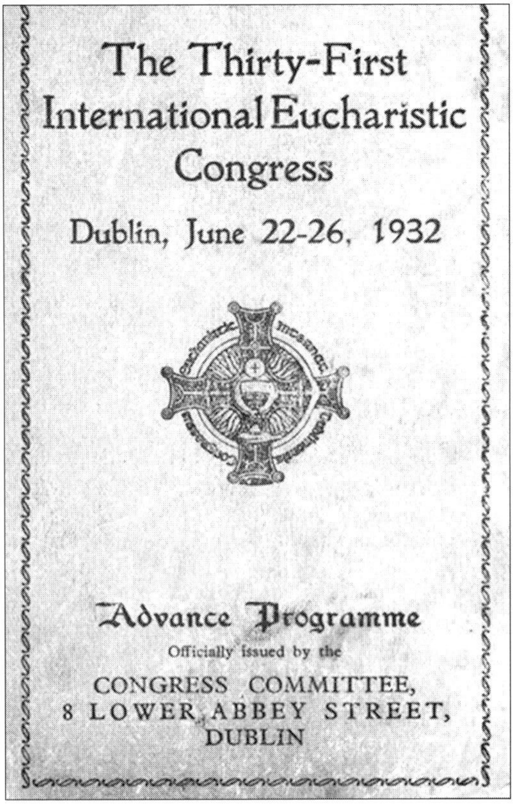

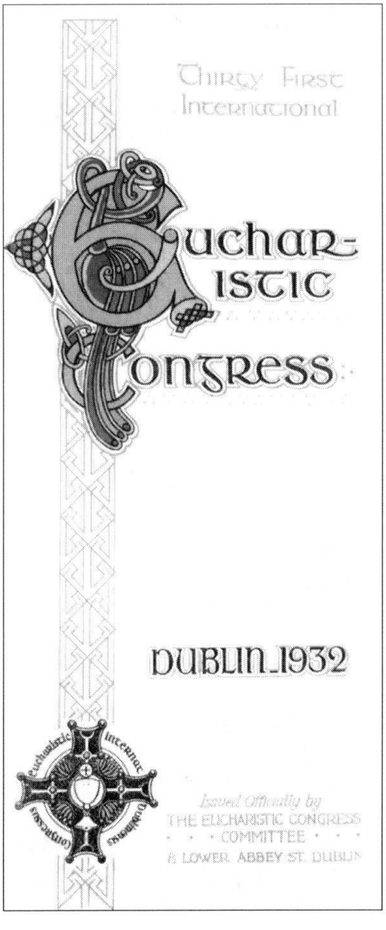

Above: Such was the demand for information that this detailed advance programme was published one year before the Congress. (*Courtesy of Dublin Diocesan Archives, Eucharistic Congress Collection.*)

Right: Eucharistic Congress Programme of Events. (*Courtesy of Dublin Diocesan Archives, Eucharistic Congress Collection.*)

Replica Round Tower at College Green. (*Courtesy of Dublin Diocesan Archives.*)

Around Ireland

The following newspaper article, from the *Derry Journal*, 25 September 1932, illustrates the extent to which the Congress was a national celebration embraced all over the country:

Clonmany's Profession of Faith

It is only what might be expected that Clonmany [situated on the Inishowen Peninsula], which is one of the most Catholic parishes in Ireland, should not be lacking in its public demonstration of welcome and loyalty to the Papal Legate. Accordingly decorations started on Friday afternoon and by Saturday evening the countryside was simply transformed. Arches of streamers, bunting and flags bearing the Papal and Eucharistic designs floated all over the parish. The houses, right to Leenan Head, vied with one another as to which should display the greatest taste and originality in decoration. A beautiful shrine is erected outside Fr Maguire's residence.

On news being received through the wireless on Monday that the Papal Legate had landed in Dublin, willing boys set forth for the hills, and from Dunaff Hill, Rachtan Mor and Bulaba, a regular conflagration ascended to the skies. The bonfire on the highest peak of Bulaba was especially attractive, forming a star-like beacon between Clonmany and Dublin, and reminiscent of St Patrick's fire of 1,500 years ago.

The sodality band was requisitioned and a procession formed at St Maeliosa's Hall and followed by an immense crowd, proceeded to the town singing hymns. On arriving at the tar barrels, the assembly knelt around and said the Rosary for the success of the Congress in Irish. The singing of

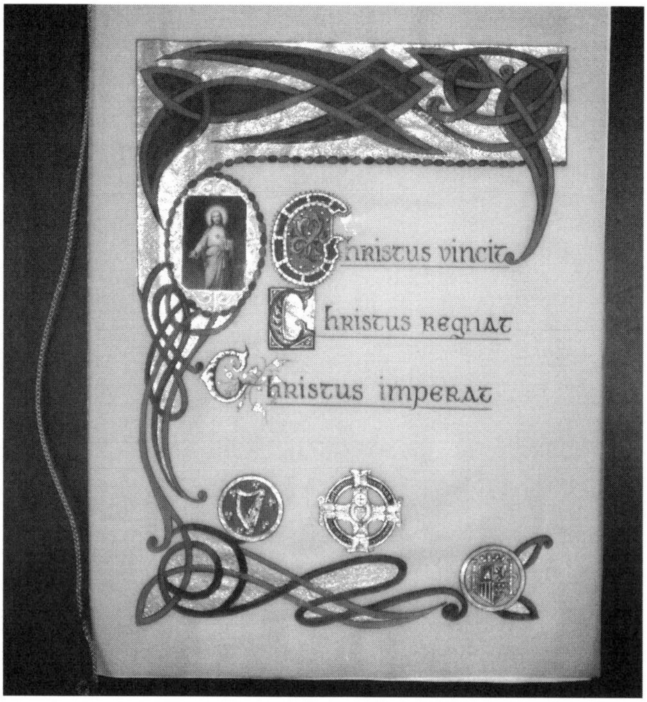

One of the many 'Spiritual Bouquets' received at the Archbishop's House. (*Courtesy of Dublin Diocesan Archives, Eucharistic Congress Collection.*)

hymns was continued until the early hours of Tuesday morning.

A repetition of same was held last night and will be repeated on Sunday night. So adept have the young men become at illuminating that they can now set the heather ablaze so that E.C., the initials of the great Congress, can be readily distinguished with as much accuracy as if the flood lights of electricity were being concentrated on the hillside.

***

The Congress was organised and sponsored by the Catholic Church in Ireland. The funding was principally provided by special church collections throughout the country which began in 1930. At the request of the organising committee, various business people and firms contributed generously to the Congress. Messrs Arthur Guinness, Son & Co. Ltd subscribed £1,000, the Great Southern and the Great Northern Railways each contributed £500, the Alliance and Dublin Gas Company contributed £250, to name but a few. It was estimated that the total cost of organising the Congress was a mere £77,925 11*s* 2*d* (excluding the state expenditure on the Congress). There was indeed a credit balance from the collections of £5,421 14*s*. The extraordinary voluntary contribution along with the state support must be appreciated here. It should also be remembered that the Congress impacted very positively on the Irish economy, however briefly. It was later reported that £5,000,000 was spent in the Free State during the Congress (National Archives, DFA 35/50).

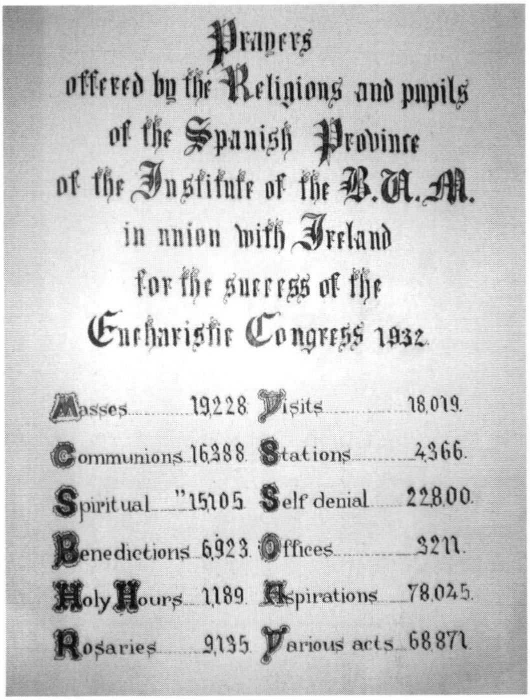

Inside the same bouquet (facing page). (*Courtesy of Dublin Diocesan Archives.*)

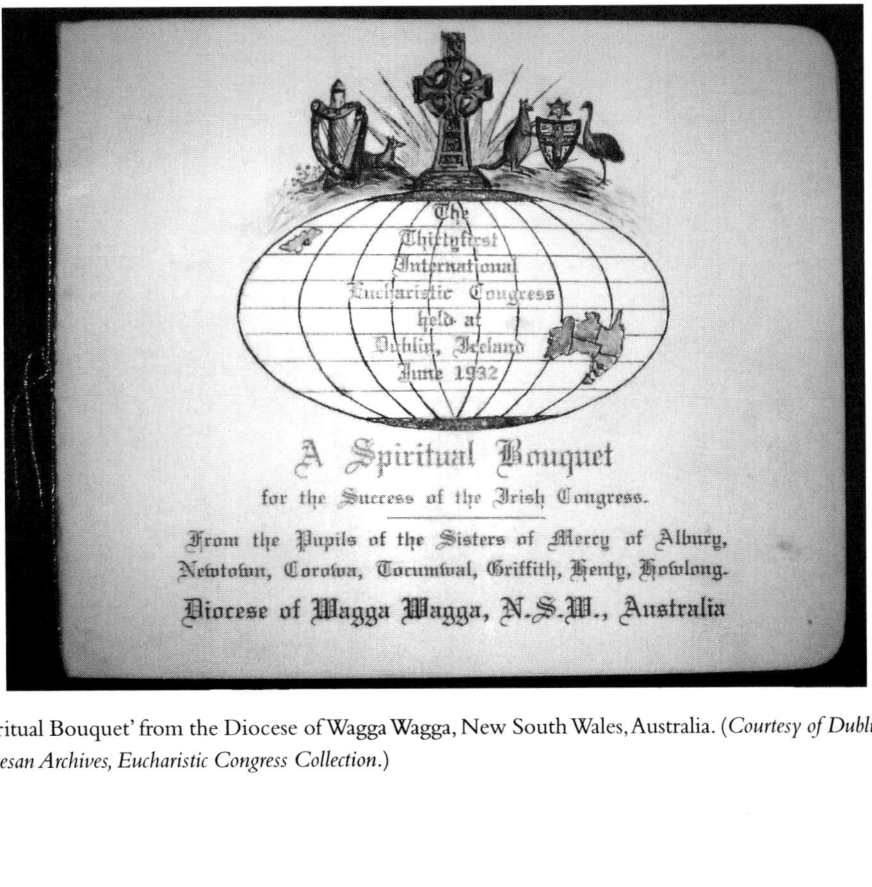

'Spiritual Bouquet' from the Diocese of Wagga Wagga, New South Wales, Australia. (*Courtesy of Dublin Diocesan Archives, Eucharistic Congress Collection.*)

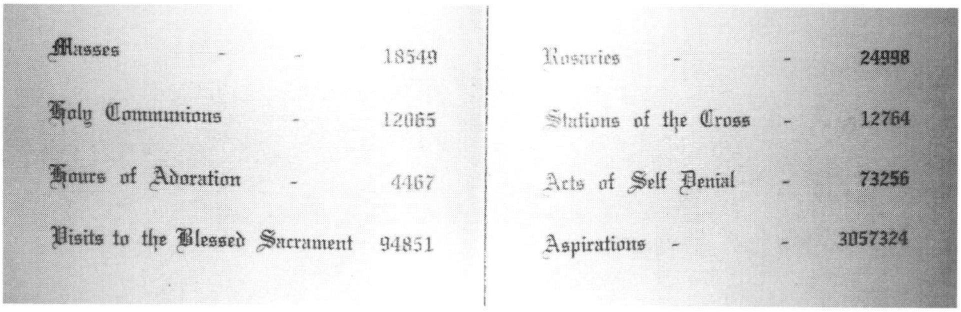

Masses	- -	18549	Rosaries	- -	24998
Holy Communions	-	12065	Stations of the Cross	-	12764
Hours of Adoration	-	4467	Acts of Self Denial	-	73256
Visits to the Blessed Sacrament		94851	Aspirations	- -	3057324

The bouquet from the Diocese of Wagga Wagga (inside). (*Courtesy of Dublin Diocesan Archives, Eucharistic Congress Collection.*)

Institute of the Good Shepherd
Evere – Brussels
Belgium

The Handmaids of the Blessed Sacrament have prayed fervently for the best result of the Eucharistic days of Dublin and they as of Your Excellenca the highest blessing.

Spiritual Flowers

H. Masses	997	Rosaries	2357
H. Communions	979	Hours of silence	893
Spir. Communions	4898	Acts of Charity	508
Sacrifices	5963		

'Spiritual Bouquet' from Brussels. (*Courtesy of Dublin Diocesan Archives, Eucharistic Congress Collection.*)

Decorations in Blackpool, Cork. (*Courtesy of Dublin Diocesan Archives, Eucharistic Congress Collection.*)

Decorative Arch, Athlunkard Street, Limerick. (*Courtesy of Denis O'Shaughnessy.*)

Decorations on Baker Street, Cullingtree Road, West Belfast. The banner in the foreground reads, 'Hail Mary, Bless the Congress.' Notice the twin spires of St Peter's Cathedral in the background. (*Courtesy of Dublin Diocesan Archives, Eucharistic Congress Collection.*)

Congress decorations in Carndonagh, Co. Donegal. (*Courtesy of Dublin Diocesan Archives, Eucharistic Congress Collection.*)

Congress decorations in King Street, Wexford. (*Courtesy of Dublin Diocesan Archives, Eucharistic Congress Collection.*)

Decorative Arch in Derry. (*Courtesy of Dublin Diocesan Archives, Eucharistic Congress Collection.*)

Decorations in Castleblaney, Co. Monaghan. (*Courtesy of Dublin Diocesan Archives, Eucharistic Congress Collection.*)

Benediction of the Blessed Sacrament taking place outside the General Post Office, Sligo, following a Eucharistic Congress procession in which over 10,000 people had participated. Such scenes were taking place in many Irish towns and cities during the Congress. (*Courtesy of Dublin Diocesan Archives, Eucharistic Congress Collection.*)

Sullivan and Downey families gathered around Congress shrine at Ahabeg Cross on the Beara Peninsula, West Cork. Shrines such as this were to be seen throughout rural Ireland during the Congress. (*Courtesy of Beara Historical Society*.)

***

The Irish Diaspora

The Congress also highlighted the remarkable number and status of Irish ecclesiastics serving both the Irish diaspora and countless others in many different parts of the world. Among those who participated in the Congress was the Waterford-born Archbishop of Sydney, Michael Kelly, who had sponsored an international Eucharistic Congress in his adopted city in 1928. Many Irish people would have been aware of other Irish ecclesiastics (Daniel Mannix, Patrick Clune, James Duhig, Robert Spence, etc.) who dominated the Catholic Church hierarchy in Australia at this time. Similarly, most of the dominant figures in the Catholic Church in the United States were either Irish-born or of immediate Irish descent. The Archbishop of New York, Cardinal Hayes, was one of those who travelled over for the Congress. Like others he journeyed around the country, creating great interest and excitement. He received a tumultuous welcome when he visited his mother's native place near Killarney. Unprecedented crowds filled the magnificent Cathedral and grounds at Killarney when he said Mass there, stirring the crowd when he spoke emotionally of his pride in his Kerry roots. The Archbishop of Boston, Cardinal O'Connell, both of whose parents were Irish emigrants and the Archbishop of Philadelphia, Cardinal Dougherty, whose parents had emigrated from Mayo, were two other 'Princes of the Church' who travelled to

The Archbishop of New York, Cardinal Hayes. (*Courtesy of Dublin Diocesan Archives, Eucharistic Congress Collection.*)

Ireland for the Congress together with numerous other notable Irish-American prelates, all of whom appear to have received very warm receptions when visiting their native places (or those of their parents) around the country.

A significant number of Irish missionary priests and bishops serving in Africa, India, China, the Philippines and elsewhere also participated in the Congress. The Bishop of Abila, Joseph Shanahan (C.S.Sp.), who had directed the building of schools, hospitals, mission stations and teachers' colleges in Western Nigeria for thirty years, attended. An equally inspirational missionary figure who attended the Congress was Thomas Broderick (SMA), Bishop of Western Nigeria. Irish missionary institutions had been assigned vicariates in many parts of Africa in particular. Fr John Heffernan travelled to Ireland from Africa to be consecrated Bishop of Uzzpari and Vicar Apostolic of Zanzibar (Tanzania) just three days before the Congress officially began. The consecration took place in the chapel at Blackrock College, where both he and one of his former school friends, Éamon de Valera, had been students. The consecration was attended by many state dignitaries, including de Valera.

***

The International Dimension

The Eucharistic Congress provided the setting for the creation of international contacts between two related families – the O'Rourkes of Ireland and those of Poland. Present at the Congress was Bishop Edward O'Rourke of Danzig (now Gdansk in Poland). O'Rourke had been nominated by the Pope as Bishop of Danzig in 1925, following the creation of the diocese around the Free City of Danzig (split between Germany and Poland). His family were of Irish ancestry, descended from exiles who had left Ireland in the 1690s after the Battle of the Boyne. In Russia they became an aristocratic family, holding high office under the Tsars, retaining the hereditary title of 'Count'. Born in Minsk, in present-day Belarus, Bishop O'Rourke was conscious of his Irish roots, and visited Ireland in the early years of the century. At the Congress he met with Senator Bernard O'Rourke and the two established a strong relationship, enjoying their shared family heritage. After the Congress, Senator O'Rourke visited Bishop O'Rourke in Danzig. Later, following Bishop O'Rourke's flight from Poland, Senator O'Rourke lobbied the Irish Government to have the Bishop admitted to Ireland as a refugee, but was unsuccessful.

As a relative of Senator O'Rourke further explained to the author, at the end of the Second World War, members of Bishop O'Rourke's family came to Britain and Ireland from Poland as refugees (some having experienced the concentration camps), and contact was renewed with the Irish O'Rourkes.

Among the many non-Irish prelates visiting for the Congress were the Catholic Primate of Poland, Cardinal Hlond; the Archbishop of Malines (Belgium), Cardinal Van Roey; the Archbishop of Palermo, Cardinal Lavitrano; Archbishop Jansen, Catholic Primate of Holland; and the Archbishop of Paris, Cardinal Verdier. The Superior-Generals of various Catholic religious orders were also present, along with numerous other archbishops and bishops from around the globe (See Appendix).

The oldest bishop in the world, Archbishop Redwood of Wellington, New Zealand, who

Above: Éamon de Valera with Bishop Joseph Heffernan, June 1932. (*Courtesy of Dublin Diocesan Archives, Eucharistic Congress Collection.*)

Left: Bishop Edward O'Rourke of Danzig.

was approaching his ninety-fourth birthday, attended the Congress. Redwood, who had been ordained in Maynooth College in 1865 and who had taught in the Marist Colleges in Dundalk and in Dublin, had always been particularly inspired by the story of St Patrick (he had also been consecrated bishop at his special request on St Patrick's Day 1874) and as a result had a fervent desire to be in Dublin to celebrate the great anniversary. Journalists were struck by his sturdy frame, his bronzed and virtually unlined face, and his kindly humour. (The youngest archbishop in the world Revd Dr Tonna, Archbishop of Smyrna (Asia Minor) also attended the Congress.)

Among the many other notable visitors was the great intellectual and theologian Père Gillet, Master General of the Dominican Order and a member of the Permanent Committee of Eucharistic Congresses. Gillet had produced many works of outstanding merit. Another notable Church intellectual was Fulton Sheen – yet another visiting Churchman returning to his Irish roots – who was then presenting a very popular weekly radio broadcast in the US, *The Catholic Hour*, which would later have a weekly listening audience of 4 million people. He would go on to present the first religious service broadcast on the new medium of television, drawing as many as 30 million people on a weekly basis. In Dublin in 1932 Sheen gave an address, 'Calvary on Irish Altars', at a meeting of the American group in the Mansion House and was very well received.

One of the most striking visitors for the Congress must have been Fr Philip Gordon of the Chippewa Tribe, Wisconsin, who attracted much friendly attention as he proudly donned his highly impressive honorary ceremonial headdress. Gordon (whose real name could be translated as 'Sign in the Sky') was a full-blooded Native American Indian who had converted to Catholicism, and had later trained for the priesthood. As Chesterton noted, 'he walked about in the streets with his tremendous tiara of plumes towering up like a grove of palm trees. Under that was the unmistakeable high-featured face moulded in copper; the red relentless mask of our boyhood dreams.' Gordon, a gregarious and cheerful priest, took the time to visit many children in hospitals throughout the city and one can easily imagine how enthralled young children would have been to meet him. Another person captivated was Éamon de Valera, who invited Fr Gordon to his office in Government Buildings. In October 1919, while on a political tour of the US, de Valera visited Wisconsin and while there he was made honorary chief of a Chippewa tribe of Indians at the Chippewa Reservation, where he too was pictured donning a ceremonial headdress. De Valera was probably already acquainted with Fr Gordon from that visit.

Among the other highly noticeable pilgrims were some of those travelling from the Orient. Again Chesterton was driven to record that he met one 'dignified Indian gentleman' who:

> ...had changed his neighbours by bringing them back into the Roman Communion; but he had changed in nothing else. By the look of him, he might have walked that moment out of any Hindoo temple covered with bulbous imagery, or any Persian mosque scrawled with a fantastic script. He wore a sort of a tall turban for a mitre; his keen and vigilant face looked browner and darker behind his grey luxuriant beard; his vestments were of a cut and pattern new to all the Western World. At the first careless glance, he might have been anything; the private chaplain of Genghis Khan or the High Priest of the cult of the Holy Monkey or the Sacred Snake. For we in Europe are generally very vague about distinguishing one Asiatic dress or dignity from another. Only, in his hand he carried something that was not the sign of the snake or the ape, or any wild cult of the sort that had

Above left: Archbishop of Wellington, Revd Dr Francis Redwood. (*Courtesy of Dublin Diocesan Archives, Eucharistic Congress Collection*.)
Above right: Fulton Sheen
Below: Fr Gordon at the Cappagh Hospital, Finglas. (*Courtesy of Dublin Diocesan Archives, Eucharistic Congress Collection*.)

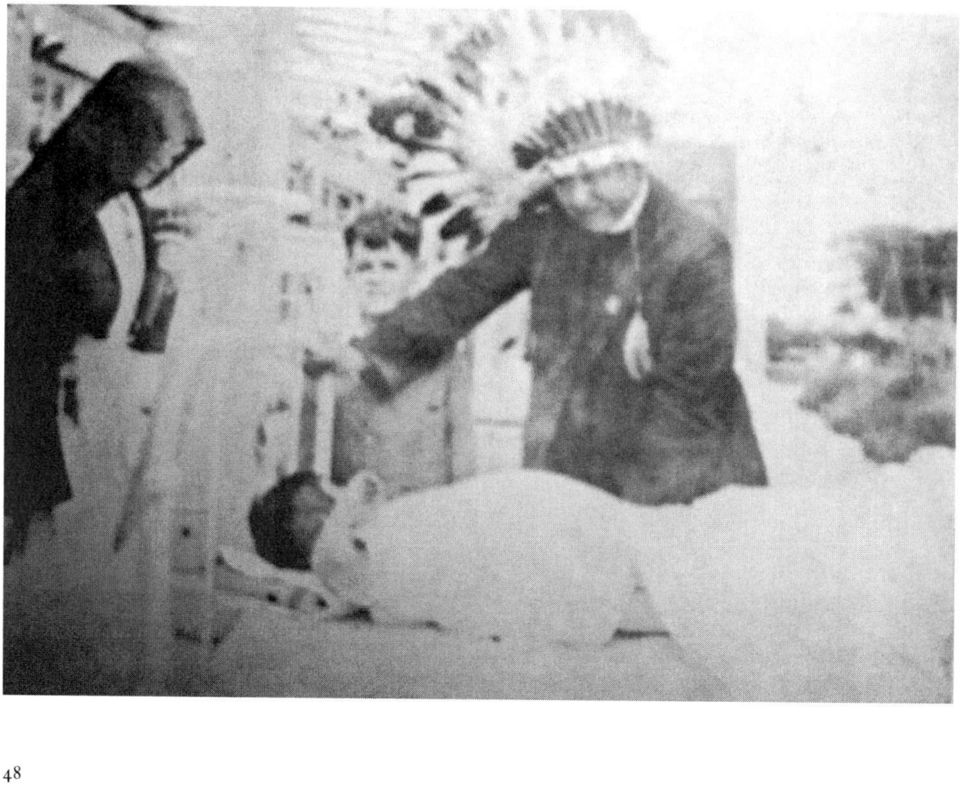

perhaps surrounded it for centuries; it was the strange sign that was once the shape of the Roman gibbet and still represented to him the divine paradox of Rome.

(*Christendom in Dublin*, pp24–25.)

Other exotic-looking Churchmen, such as those of the Eastern Rite (as opposed to the Latin Rite) coming from Greece, Cyprus and elsewhere, with their elaborate vestments, 'strange' liturgical practices and typically large beards, also captured the imagination and interest of a thoroughly engaged Dublin public.

***

Fr Gordon of the Chippewa Tribe, Wisconsin. (*Courtesy of Dublin Diocesan Archives, Eucharistic Congress Collection.*)

The Archbishop of Bethany (India), Revd Dr Mar Ivanios – the source of Chesterton's fascination – was the founder of the Bethany Ashram order of monks. He had been ordained a bishop of the Malankara Syriac Orthodox Church in 1908 and later led an attempt at the reunion of the Malankara Church with the Roman Catholic Church. He has often been nicknamed the 'Newman of the East'. Shortly before the Congress in Dublin he was named Archbishop of Trivandrum and received the pallium from Pope Pius XI. He is also renowned for his pioneering efforts in the fields of education and dedication to the cause of the poor. Efforts continue for his canonisation. (*Courtesy of Dublin Diocesan Archives, Eucharistic Congress Collection.*)

Oriental pilgrims at the Congress. (*Courtesy of Dublin Diocesan Archives, Eucharistic Congress Collection.*)

The celebrants of the Pontifical Liturgy in the Slavic Rite at St Francis Xavier's church: Mgr Bucys (left), Mgr Herbingy (centre) and Mgr Czarnicki (right). (*Courtesy of Dublin Diocesan Archives, Eucharistic Congress Collection.*)

The Archbishop of Paris, Cardinal Verdier (centre), photographed outside the tenement dwelling where Matt Talbot had lived in Rutland Street. (*Courtesy of Dublin Diocesan Archives, Eucharistic Congress Collection.*)

Dublin's Devotional Cults

One of the many striking aspects of the Congress was the way in which visitors quickly absorbed local cults of devotion. Hundreds (if not thousands) visited the grave of the pious Dublin labourer Matt Talbot, whose remains were then buried in Glasnevin Cemetery. The Archbishop of Paris, Cardinal Verdier, was one of the many who developed a particular interest in Matt Talbot. During a crowded French sectional Mass in the University church, St Stephen's Green, he described with considerable emotion his experience looking for the tenement house where Talbot had lived in the north inner city:

> Yesterday I had the most soul-thrilling experience of my life. In this quarter I saw the balconies crowded with men and women poorly clad. I saw an altar erected and decorated with pictures of many saints of heaven – an altar erected by workmen to honour God in the Holy Eucharist. I knelt on a *prie-dieu* never meant for a Cardinal of the Church, on it I offered up the best prayer of my life. My eyes were filled with tears. Workmen, women, children, crowded around me in such numbers that were it not for the kindly policemen and Boy Scouts I might never have got away with my life.
>
> I mounted the stairs of a humble dwelling, and found in a room a poor woman to whom unfortunately I could not make myself understood, but whose eyes manifested the joy of her heart to see a 'Prince of the Church' offering his prayers to her own brother, Matt Talbot, to the Irishman who rivals St Benedict in his spirit of loyalty to Christ.

The crowd of people who gathered around the house on hearing the Cardinal was visiting. (*Courtesy of Dublin Diocesan Archives, Eucharistic Congress Collection.*)

'The Irish Lourdes' Grotto, Inchicore. (*Courtesy of Tony Behan.*)

Thousands of visiting pilgrims also travelled out to see the Lourdes Grotto (a full-scale replica of the original) erected in the grounds of the Oblate Fathers' House of Retreat, Inchicore. Although only two years in existence it was estimated that some half a million people visited the grotto up to the time of the Congress. The solemn opening of the grotto in May 1930 represented one of the greatest religious demonstrations ever witnessed in Dublin and thousands flocked to see 'the Irish Lourdes' during the Congress. The Bishop of Lourdes, Revd Dr Gerlier, was one of those particularly interested. He was a guest (along with six other prelates) of the Superior-General of the Oblate Order in Ireland, Fr Sweeney, in the Oblate Retreat House, adjacent to the Inchicore Grotto. Fr Sweeney was so proud of the decorative efforts of the residents of Inchicore that he took Bishop Gerlier on a special tour of the district, again creating great excitement among the locals.

Ecce Sacerdos Magnus

The major guest of the state was the visiting Papal Legate Cardinal Lorenzo Lauri – who immediately became a focal point for displays of devotion from his arrival in Ireland, amid memorable scenes of pomp and sheer exuberance, on 20 June. The Cardinal Legate was accompanied by a pontifical mission which included a member of the Secretariat of State to the Vatican, Francis Spellman, who was of Irish descent and who would later become archbishop of New York. Among the other members of the mission were Monsignor Curran, Rector of the Irish College in Rome; Count Dalla Torre, Director of the *Osservatore Romano*; Monsignor Calderari, the Pontifical Master of Ceremonies, and two magnificently uniformed Chamberlains of the Cape and Sword, Monsignors Croci and Vignoli. The mission travelled to Ireland via France and Great Britain (where they were met by representatives of the archbishop of Dublin and the Saorstát High Commissioner in London, James Dulanty), receiving a jubilant welcome by Irish émigrés in London before setting off by train to Chester (where they spent the night) and then on to Holyhead the following morning. At Holyhead the mission boarded the SS *Cambria* for the final stage of their journey to Dublin.

Shortly before 3p.m. the SS *Cambria* was in sight of Dún Laoghaire Harbour. A battery of guns were mounted at the end of the East Pier and a nineteen-gun artillery salute (a royal salute) was fired and the guns boomed at regular intervals until the ship entered the harbour. By this stage very large crowds had gathered all around. It was a glorious sunny afternoon and the harbour and town of Dún Laoghaire were beautifully decorated. The Papal Legate's boat was led from the Kish Lighthouse into the harbour mouth by a squadron of Irish Air Corps planes (Avro 631s) flying in cross formation overhead. Numerous boats had come out from Howth and elsewhere to form a colourful convoy for the *Cambria* as it made its way into the harbour.

The military on the Carlisle Pier (where the landing stage for ships in the harbour is situated) were formed into two files as the Guard of Honour. The Army No. 1 Band was also stationed on the pier. After the boat had moored, a group of dignitaries made their way up the red-carpeted gangway to be received by the Papal Legate in the saloon of the ship. Among those who boarded the ship were the Archbishop of Dublin, President de Valera

The Papal Legate, Cardinal Lorenzo Lauri. (*Courtesy of Dublin Diocesan Archives, Eucharistic Congress Collection.*)

The Pontifical Mission before setting off from the Vatican. (*Courtesy of Dublin Diocesan Archives, Eucharistic Congress Collection.*)

The SS *Cambria* entering Dún Laoghaire Harbour, escorted by aeroplanes flying in cross formation. (*Courtesy of Dublin Diocesan Archive, Eucharistic Congress Collection.*)

Papal Legate blessing the Guard of Honour after disembarking at Dún Laoghaire. Éamon de Valera can be seen to the left of the Legate and Archbishop Byrne to the right. (*Courtesy of Dublin Diocesan Archives, Eucharistic Congress Collection.*)

Crowds gathered outside Dún Laoghaire Train Station (now Hartley's Restaurant) to welcome the Papal Legate. Notice the Catholic Boy Scouts controlling the crowds. Some 4,000 Scouts, from all over Ireland, assisted with great efficiency at various stewarding duties during the Congress. (*Courtesy of Dublin Diocesan Archives, Eucharistic Congress Collection.*)

and other government ministers (whom the Legate originally presumed to be detectives as they were not in formal dress), members of various Congress committees and the Dún Laoghaire Borough Corporation – two members of whom read an address of welcome in Irish and English to the Legate (against the advice of the Government). A short time later the Legate disembarked from the ship amid rapturous cheering and applause, which continued as he walked the distance of 180 yards to the open motor car in which he was to travel. The Garda Band played the new Papal anthem 'Inno Pontificio'. The Guard of Honour, the infantry battalion and the members of the Gardaí who lined the route to the motor car, along with the magnificent Mounted Escort (which was formed outside the Royal St George Yacht Club) with swords rendered, all saluted as the Legate passed. It was estimated that approximately 50,000 people gathered around the harbour to greet him. The Legate acknowledged the extraordinary greeting he was receiving, motioning his hand again and again in blessing.

When the Legate reached the car, where he would be accompanied by the Archbishop of Dublin and the President, a section of the Mounted Escort led the procession towards the city, the other section following immediately behind the Legate's car, further followed by a procession of sixty cars. The procession made its way from Crofton Road along the coastal route by which the Legate could enjoy the spectacular view of Dublin Bay coming up from

William Donnelly, Captain of the Mounted Escort, resplendent in full uniform of light-blue tunic with gold frogging and lace, breeches and dark Sealskin busby with orange-yellow plumes. (*Courtesy of William Donnelly Jr.*)

The Mounted Escort in formation outside the Royal St George Yacht Club, Dún Laoghaire, on the arrival of the Papal Legate. It was the first public appearance of the Escort, which continued in existence until 1948 when ceremonial escort duties were handed over to the motorcyclists of the Cavalry Corps. (*Courtesy of William Donnelly Jr.*)

The Papal Legate passing through the 'City Gates' at Merrion with the Blue Hussars (as the Mounted Escort were popularly known) in the background. (*Courtesy of Dublin Diocesan Archives, Eucharistic Congress Collection.*)

Longford Terrace. Hundreds of young children (with schools closed for the occasion) lined the route to Blackrock. Teachers, parents, stewards, Boy Scouts and Girl Guides were at hand to ensure order and safety. To Dublin mothers in particular (regardless of how poor they may have been), it appeared to be absolutely paramount that that their children would be well dressed for the Congress events and pictures prove emphatically just how successful they were in this endeavour. Virtually every child would have had a miniature flag to wave as the procession passed. Every vantage point was filled by people through Blackrock and along the Rock Road.

At Merrion, the city boundary was indicated by two great ornamental pylons (representative of an ancient City Gate). Here the procession came to a halt and the Legate was welcomed by the Lord Mayor of Dublin, Alfie Byrne and other city aldermen dressed in their ceremonial robes. The Lord Mayor had travelled out to the boundary in his stately gold-embellished coach, which was gleaming in the sunshine. The coach had special associations with Daniel O'Connell, the first Catholic Lord Mayor of Dublin since the Reformation. A platform had been erected at the boundary where the Lord Mayor made an address of welcome indicating the loyalty of so many civic leaders in the state to a representative of the Pope:

> In the august person of Your Eminence we welcome not merely the distinguished Cardinal, chosen Legate of the Pope, but also and especially we reverently greet the Vicar of Jesus Christ himself. For to us, Catholics of Dublin and Irishmen, your Eminence is another Patrick, messenger of grace and communion with the Holy See. In your eminence we gladly recognise the living image of the Church which is One because of the supreme authority of the successor of St Peter. To your eminence, then, we pay, as to Our Most Holy Father, Pius XI, full tribute of dutiful submission, filial love, and grateful Faith. Welcome to your Eminence, Legate of His Holiness, a hundred thousand welcomes to you, in whom we have the honour to salute the successor of St Peter, the Vicar of Christ Himself.

Following a further address by the City Manager in Irish, English and Latin, the Cardinal Legate was presented with the address of welcome printed on vellum with beautiful surrounding ornamentation based on the style of the Book of Kells. Then, speaking in English, the Legate finally had opportunity to express his appreciation:

> Please accept my heartfelt thanks, my dear Lord Mayor, for the cordial welcome that you, together with the aldermen and members of the Dublin City Council, have accorded me in the name of the citizens of Dublin.
>
> I feel honoured to be the Pontifical Legate of His Holiness, Pope Pius XI, and to preside as his ambassador at the Thirty First International Eucharistic Congress now about to begin in this historic city of Dublin, the centre, the heart, and capital of Ireland so justly renowned in all the world for the strong practical faith and the special attachment to the Holy See which have ever been characteristic of her noble people.
>
> I confide the success of the Congress to Divine Providence and to the intercession of your great apostle St Patrick, who fifteen centuries ago planted so deeply the Catholic faith in Irish hearts and I join my prayers with your good wishes, so graciously expressed, that one of the results of the Congress will be the forging of new bonds of attachment between the Irish people and the Holy See.

Lord Mayor of Dublin, Alfie Byrne kissing the ring of the Papal Legate at the city boundary. (*Courtesy of Dublin Diocesan Archives, Eucharistic Congress Collection.*)

> In accordance with your desire, very willingly I shall at once communicate with the Holy Father and inform his Holiness of your sincere cordiality and exquisite kindness, and of the very warm welcome which the great and good Irish people gave to the representative of the Pope.

Between the city boundary and the Pro-Cathedral, the procession passed through an enormous crowd of people. In particular, from Mount Street Bridge onwards a solid mass of people lined both sides of the route with a continuous wave of cheering. Coming from Ballsbridge and Northumberland Road, the procession proceeded along Lower Mount Street, Merrion Square, Clare Street, Leinster Street, Nassau Street, College Green (where no doubt the Legate viewed the unmissable replica Round Tower), Westmoreland Street, O'Connell Street, Cathal Brugha Street and Marlborough Street.

On arriving outside the Pro-Cathedral the Legate made his way first to the Scoil Éinne building on the other side of the street, which was being used as robing rooms for the ceremonies in the Pro-Cathedral. As the crowds had been gathering in the area earlier, cheers had been raised for any cardinal, archbishop or bishop who was recognised crossing from the robing rooms to the Pro-Cathedral.

When the Papal Legate appeared from the robing rooms and moved slowly across the street

The Papal Legate (centre) at the platform at Merrion responding to the address of welcome from the Lord Mayor. Éamon de Valera and Alfie Byrne can be seen to the left, along with various city aldermen and councillors in ceremonial robes. Notice one of the Lord Mayor's Heralds to the right in ceremonial dress with trumpet. (*Courtesy of Tony Behan.*)

proceeded by a cross bearer and various dignitaries, most of the crowd dropped on their knees. A fanfare was sounded by trumpeters of the Municipal School of Music. Archbishop Byrne, standing at the entrance to the Pro-Cathedral along with all of the Irish hierarchy, formally received the Legate, and the procession then moved into the Cathedral.

When the Legate entered the Cathedral the Palestrina choir (accompanied by a former member, John McCormack) sang 'Ecce Sacerdos Magnus'. While the Legate knelt at the faldstool the prayer 'Omnipotens Sempiterne Deus' was sung along with the other prescribed versicles. After the choir sang the Antiphon, the Legate ascended to the altar, sang the prayer and gave his blessing to all. Throughout the ceremony loudspeakers and amplifiers carried the sounds of the hymns through the city centre and thousands knelt in prayer and thanksgiving.

At the end of the service it was announced on the loudspeakers that 'the Cardinal Legate is now leaving the Cathedral' and there was great cheering as he crossed to the robing rooms. As soon as the Legate was clad again in his travelling robes he was driven, still accompanied by a full military escort, to the Archbishop's House in Drumcondra. The route from the Pro-Cathedral to Drumcondra was even more profusely decorated than the route from Dún Laoghaire and there were even greater crowds gathered along the streets to welcome the Legate. On approaching the

A view from a rooftop on Westmoreland Street of the procession to the Pro-Cathedral. The altar on O'Connell Bridge (still surrounded by scaffolding) would be used for the final ceremony of the Congress. Nelson's Pillar (destroyed in 1966 by a bomb explosion) can be seen in the distance. The high viewing platform was bedecked with Congress flags and, with a deliberate historic irony perhaps, a large tricolour. (*Courtesy of Dublin Diocesan Archives, Eucharistic Congress Collection.*)

Archbishop's House, the Artane Boys' Band (situated outside the gates) played the Papal Hymn as two Guards of Honour (one comprising the Galway Sea Scouts) saluted the Legate. Clearly struck by the welcome he had received throughout the day the Legate entered the Archbishop's House, where he would stay for all but one night of his visit to Ireland.

On the following day the Feast of St Aloysius (Patron of Youth) was solemnised with a general communion for children throughout Ireland. An estimated 700,000 children received Holy Communion on the day and offered their communions for the success of the Congress, for the faith of Ireland and for the welfare of the Holy Father.

Later that afternoon a garden party was held in the grounds of Blackrock College by the Irish hierarchy to welcome the Legate. Great marquees had been erected in the playing fields and the occasion was attended by over 20,000 people. All of the Irish hierarchy were present, as were the Governor-General James Mac Neill, President de Valera and other government ministers, many visiting prelates, foreign visitors, hundreds of clergy and various distinguished citizens. When the Papal Legate arrived there was great applause. From a balcony overlooking the grounds he surveyed the scene in glorious sunshine. Raising his hand to bestow a blessing on the crowd it appeared that virtually everyone in the vast gathering knelt to receive his blessing. A pause followed, which was eventually broken by one

The Papal Legate singing a prayer at the welcoming ceremony at the Pro-Cathedral. Due to its relatively small size and poor location along a narrow street, the Cathedral was not an ideal venue for Congress ceremonies. Built before Catholic Emancipation, it was more representative of that era than of Ireland in 1932. Archbishop Byrne had purchased Merrion Square from the Earl of Pembroke in 1930 with the intention of building a great Cathedral that would more accurately reflect the position and influence of the Catholic Church in independent Ireland. The harsh economic conditions in the early 1930s forced the postponement of these plans. Byrne's successor, Archbishop John Charles McQuaid dismissed the plans as a waste of vital diocesan funds. (*Courtesy of Dublin Diocesan Archives, Eucharistic Congress Collection.*)

person in the crowd who began to sing 'Faith of our Fathers'. In a remarkably spontaneous gesture the entire crowd began to sing the hymn in unison. Afterwards, the Legate began to walk among the crowd (surrounded by a vigilant guard of Boy Scouts). The No. 1 Army Band, the Band of the Metropolitan Garda Síochána, and the St James Brass and Reed Band performed various numbers and great colour was added to the occasion when a large group of Dutch Girl Guides (of the Graal Association) arrived waving large banners and encouraging more singing from the crowd.

Later that evening the triduum of prayer, in final preparation for the Congress, ended with special devotions in all Dublin churches. That night another great social event in connection with the Congress took place, with the State Reception for the Papal Legate at Dublin Castle. Virtually all of the prelates and dignitaries who travelled to Dublin for the Congress attended, as did the representative section of Irish people from all classes, who were also invited. Approximately 4,000 people attended the occasion. The Legate was formally received by President de Valera, the recently elected head of Government, in St Patrick's Hall, who then proceeded with an address of welcome on behalf of the people of Saorstát Éireann. He spoke in Irish and then Latin:

Crowds gathered at North Earl Street and Talbot Street, to welcome the Papal Legate. (*Courtesy of Dublin Diocesan Archives, Eucharistic Congress Collection.*)

The Legate and his suite at the Archbishop's House in Drumcondra. (*Courtesy of Dublin Diocesan Archives, Eucharistic Congress Collection.*)

The Papal Legate, on a platform specially built for his visit, addressing the crowd at the Garden Party in Blackrock College. (*Courtesy of Dublin Diocesan Archives, Eucharistic Congress Collection.*)

Guests at the Garden Party kneeling for the Legate's blessing. (*Courtesy of Dublin Diocesan Archives, Eucharistic Congress Collection.*)

Members of the Graal Association from Holland at the Garden Party. (*Courtesy of Dublin Diocesan Archives, Eucharistic Congress Collection.*)

Míle míle fáilte romhat, a Ard-Fhlaith na hEaglaise, a fhear-ionaid an Athar Naofa, go talamh iath-ghlas na hÉireann! Mile míle fáilte romhat ón fhíoríochtar is doimhne de chroí chneasta, chineálta na nGael! La glórmhar gléghlan I stair na tire seo is ea an lá beannaithe seo. Creideamh na Róimhe a thug Pádraig Naofa dhúinn. Grá don Róimh a mhúin sé dhúinn. An chreideamh céanna agus an grá céanna, do choimeád muintir na hÉireann go beo, briomhar iad ón aimsir ársa úd go dtí an lá atá inniu ann. An creideamh céanna agus an grá céanna, a bhi ag ionradh go soilseach istigh ina gcroíthe, thug muintir na hÉireann leo iad do gach áird den chruinne cheathartha. An chreideamh céanna agus an grá céanna, coimeádfaidh muintir na hÉireann go beo, bríomhar iad, agus múinfidh do lucht díchreidimh agus ainelais iad, le cúnamh Dé, an seacht lá is an fhaid a mhairfidh an bith cé.

Míle míle fáilte romhat, arís agus arís eile, a Theachtaire uasail ó thobar beannaithe ghrásta Chríost ar an mbeatha seo-an tAthair Naofa grámhar a deirim! Seoid luachmhar imeasc seoda na cruinne is ea croí lách nádúrtha na nGael. Sea, an tseoid luachmhar seo, ba mhaith linn, án tráthnóna glórmhar seo, é do thabairt duitse, agus tríotsa don Athair Naofa grámhar, an t-aonú Pius déag, le go bhfanfadh sé i gcomhad i gcochall a dhil-chroi féin go deo na ndeor.

Translation from the Latin section of the address:

My Lord Cardinal, Your Eminence, and this audience of all Ireland and of our race throughout the world, will assuredly approve if, in this Irish hall of assembly, Your Eminence has been first saluted in our national language.

Most Eminent Lord, the records of the centuries bear eloquent testimony to that loving zeal with which the apostolic see has ever honoured our nation. That special affection was ever the more amply given, in proportion of the sufferings of Ireland. Repeatedly over more than three hundred years our people, ever firm in their allegiance to our ancestral faith and unwavering even unto death in their devotion to the See of Peter, endured in full measure unmerited trials by war, by devastation and by confiscation. They saw their most sacred rights set at naught under an unjust domination. But repeatedly also did the successors of Peter most willingly come to our aid, in the persons of Gregory XIII, Clement VIII, Paul V, Urban VIII, Innocent X and many others of the line of the Roman Pontiffs down to the present day.

Today, with no less favour and goodwill, His Holiness Pope Pius XI has turned his august regard to our country, our metropolitan city, and to this present year, a year of deep significance for our people. Here are gathered not only our Irish race, but in great numbers also other peoples of the entire world, united with us in race or in faith and unreservedly do they all share in our welcome. At this solemn time, most eminent lord, has our Holy Father decreed to send Your Eminence as his Legate to Ireland, from his city and state of the Vatican.

With all veneration, respect and rejoicing, therefore, do we, the Government of Ireland, welcome Your Eminence. By reason of our public office and its duties, it is most fitting that the Irish Government should not only assist in every way the great and solemn function of the Eucharistic Congress here in Ireland, but also should take their due part and place in its proceedings.

They have very special reason for this participation, when they recall how, by his teaching and by his repeated personal action, Pope Pius XI has rendered august service to civil society; while Your Eminence, who here represents his person and his authority, has also for many years been united with many of your students, sons of the Irish race, in the noble pursuits of scholarship and of sacred learning.

There is also for us a further cause of public rejoicing. At this time, when we welcome to Ireland this latest legation from the Eternal City, we are commemorating the apostolic mission to Ireland, given fifteen centuries ago to St Patrick, apostle of our nation. Who can fail on this day to recall to mind the utterance the apostle recorded of old in the Book of Armagh, 'Even as you are children of Christ, be you also children of Rome.'

Most notable, then, in conclusion, are these auspicious days for us, in that they have brought to our land, and into this our Irish hall of assembly, Your Eminence, Cardinal of the Holy Roman Church, Legate of the Apostolic See.

The Legate made a gracious reply and afterwards the many guests were presented to him – somewhat in the manner that the British Monarch's representative in Ireland, the Viceroy, had formerly received guests in the same venue. (Note that the contemporary representative of the Crown, the Governor-General, was not invited to the reception.) Indeed the occasion was redolent with irony as Dublin Castle had for so long represented the centre and symbol of Protestant Ascendancy power in Ireland, and some journalists could not help remarking how not so long ago a Catholic priest was more likely to be found hanging from a spike outside the walls. It was also perhaps more bitterly ironic to some that here was Éamon de Valera, a *bête noir* to many unionists in Ireland and Britain, appropriating this former loyalist citadel, where even the wonderful ceiling paintings were blatant unionist propaganda. De Valera appeared to be almost teasing out the irony in his speech where he applied a classic

The Legate (centre) replying to President de Valera's (seated to the right) address of welcome at the State Reception at Dublin Castle. (*Courtesy of Dublin Diocesan Archives, Eucharistic Congress Collection.*)

faith and fatherland interpretation of Irish history to his welcoming address and did not feel the need to speak any English. It was truly a new order.

***

This bill indicates how relatively cheap the Government's largest gesture to the Congress was in real terms (National Archives S100/1/32):

Saorstát Éireann
Total Bill for Catering at the State Reception:

3,715 guests at 2*s* 6*d* each: £464 7*s* 6*d*
Claret, sauterne and cider cups, &c. in marquee: £76 13*s* 6*d*
Special refreshments in reserved supper room: £26 13*s* 6*d*
Six winemen at 25*s* each: £7 10*s* 0*d*
Total: £575 4*s* 6*d*

***

Confronting the challenges

Although the Congress took place over five days, 'the Congress period' was legally designated as commencing on 18 June and ending on 1 July (more or less coinciding with the Cardinal Legate's entire visit). An Act was written into the Irish Statute Book to extend over this period – The Eucharistic Congress (Miscellaneous Provisions) Act, 1932 (see Appendix). This Act introduced traffic control regulations, certain exemptions for hotels and restaurants in the Dublin area and numerous other special arrangements and provisions. It was a remarkable piece of legislation, which permitted the use of unlicenced motor cars on public roads, as well as permitting persons without driving licences to drive, during the 'Congress period' (see section 4 and 6 of the Act). It was a striking expression of the extent of state support for the Congress – whatever about the aforementioned financial stringency. It is worth noting here also that, at the request of Archbishop Byrne, the Minister for Justice sanctioned the release of thirty prisoners who were either first offenders or whose sentences had almost expired, as an 'Act of Grace' for the Congress.

All efforts were made to confront the short-term accommodation crisis caused by massive numbers of people travelling to Dublin for the Congress, most especially from other parts of Ireland (a vastly increased train and bus service also had to be provided to facilitate this great movement of people). Large camps were established in Cabra and Artane. Emergency accommodation was provided in numerous national schools, town halls and even library buildings in the greater Dublin area. Catering centres were set up in key city-centre locations. Mattresses were produced on a very large scale in advance of the Congress to facilitate countless Dublin households to accommodate visiting relatives and, where possible, other Congress pilgrims. A major campaign was made by the Congress organisers to encourage people to provide accommodation to visiting pilgrims. Leaflets with a cover page image of St Joseph and Our Lady seeking a lodging in Bethlehem and titled with 'You will not refuse' were distributed throughout Dublin well before the Congress and extensive surveys were carried out on the availability of accommodation. Many visiting prelates stayed with Dublin families while attending the Congress. All possible accommodation in convents and other religious houses in and around Dublin was also provided.

For some who travelled from abroad, particularly those from America, the liners in which they had travelled served as 'floating hotels' during the Congress. The numerous liners docked or moored in Alexandra Basin, Sir John Rogerson's Quay and out in Dublin Bay excited the insatiable curiosity of Dublin people over the period and added to the sense of occasion – making a particularly beautiful sight when lit up on the warm summer nights.

Éamon de Valera was one of those to have made a courtesy call to one of the liners. In this case it was the SS *Lapland* and he was returning a visit from the Archbishop of Philadelphia, Cardinal Dougherty, to his office at Government Buildings (one of many prelates and dignitaries who visited him there during the Congress). There was some irony in the fact that in 1919, not long after escaping from Lincoln Jail, de Valera was secretly smuggled upon the same ship in Liverpool and hidden 'in the bottom of the ship, rat-infested but free from detectives' before eventually obtaining quarters in the lamplighter's cabin on his way to New

A Congress Camp at Artane where some 2,000 members of the Knights of St Columba from Scotland camped. In the foreground can be seen an altar in front of which a very large congregation gathered for Midnight Mass on the opening night of the Congress. (*O'Reilly Collection.*)

York to gather support for the independence struggle in Ireland. Thirteen years later, Fr Pat O'Shea of Philadelphia, an old friend of de Valera, accompanied him on board the ship once again.

The following liners were anchored in Dublin Bay:

Doric (Alexandra Quay)
Duchess of Bedford (Alexandra Quay)
De Grasse (Alexandra Basin)
Sierra Cordoba (Alexandra Basin)
Dresden (Alexandra Basin)
Rio Bravo (Crossberth)
Marnix van Sint Aldegonde (Sir John Rogerson's Quay)
Lapland (Dublin Bay)

A Congress catering camp in the grounds of the O'Brien Institute at Marino. This was one of a number of such camps around the city to provide basic and very cheap sustenance to Congress pilgrims. The Casino Marino can be seen to the far right and the St Vincent de Paul church in the foreground. (*O'Reilly Collection*.)

Laconia (Dublin Bay)
Saturnia (Dublin Bay)
Samaria (Dublin Bay)
Antonia (Dublin Bay)

In all, fifty-eight ships were berthed at the quays during the Congress, not including the five liners out in the Bay. Dublin Port was never busier and somehow normal port operations continued through the period while the 'Congress' shipping was provided with various special services. It was an excellent achievement by the Dublin Port Authority.

***

Thousands of Dubliners would have strolled down the City Quays to view the liners. This picture captures the very cheerful atmosphere and the excellent weather. (*O'Reilly Collection.*)

The Port Tug *Coliemore* towing the 20,000-ton liner *Duchess of Bedford* (bringing Congress pilgrims from Canada) into Dublin Harbour. (*Courtesy of Niall Dardis, Dublin Port Archives.*)

The *Sierra Cordoba* and the *Dresden* moored in Alexandra Basin. (*Courtesy of Niall Dardis, Dublin Port Archives.*)

The *Royal Iris* was a tug used to convey passengers from liners in Dublin Bay into the city. It was also used during the Congress as an excursion boat whereby Dubliners could go out to see the liners in the Bay. It was one of five tenders used to ferry passengers to their ships. A Dublin Port building close by was used for the purposes of celebrating Mass for the passengers, in the absence of a church in the immediate area. (*Courtesy of Niall Dardis, Dublin Port Archives.*)

When Italian passengers on board the *Saturnia* arrived at Cobh (*en route* for Dublin) they were welcomed by the Lord Mayor of Cork, representatives of various civic bodies and members of the armed forces along with very large crowds. They had not even arrived in Dublin yet. (*Courtesy of Niall Dardis, Dublin Port Archives.*)

Foreign Sectional Meetings

As befitting any great Congress, there was also an extremely informative and intellectual side to the events. Numerous articles and essays, as well as a book, were written about St Patrick. Public lectures, most particularly relating to the Eucharist and Ireland, took place, usually in front of packed audiences, in the Theatre Royal, the Savoy Theatre, the Mansion House and University College Dublin (then situated mainly in Earlsfort Terrace). UCD provided an ideal meeting place for the many sectional groups of Congress pilgrims (groups from Portugal, Mexico, Uruguay, France, Malta, Poland, Holland, Belgium, Czechoslovakia, Spain, Italy, Lithuania, Australia, New Zealand, Canada, 'the Oriental group', etc.). These meetings included an address frequently focusing on Irish connections with a particular country and the work of Irish missionaries in that country, etc. An exhibition in the college on Irish Catholic Education, presumably directed towards the visiting pilgrims, represented an emphatic demonstration of pride in Irish Catholic history. The old UCD building in St Stephen's Green featured another very significant exhibition on Irish missionary work, intended to further stimulate public interest in mission work – especially in the work of contemporary Irish missions. Vast numbers of people visited the exhibition and given that the number of men and women who dedicated themselves to missionary work would increase substantially over the next couple of decades, it seems reasonable to speculate that this exhibition may have been an inspiration to many.

The various foreign sectional groups also needed the use of Dublin churches to celebrate Mass in their own language or as a group. Fortunately there were enough fine churches in the city to meet the challenge. The French group celebrated Mass in the beautiful University

University College Dublin building at Earlsfort Terrace. This was a very important meeting place for the foreign sectional groups visiting for the Congress. Apparently summer exams at the University finished well ahead of the normal schedule to ensure the pilgrims could have full use of the lecture halls, etc. (*Courtesy of Dublin Diocesan Archives, Eucharistic Congress Collection.*)

church, St Stephen's Green. The American group celebrated mass in St Andrew's church, Westland Row. Parishioners at St Francis Xavier's church in Gardiner Street were absorbed by Mass celebrated in the Slavonic Rite, with young Irish altar servers specially trained to assist in the ceremony.

***

Where the Cardinals Stayed

Cardinal Lauri, the Papal Legate, was the guest of the Archbishop of Dublin.
Cardinal Bourne, Archbishop of Westminster, stayed at the Sacred Heart Convent, Mount Anville.
Cardinal Verdier, Archbishop of Paris, was the guest of M. and Mme Alphand at the French Legation.
Cardinal Lavitrano, Archbishop of Palermo, stayed at the Dominican Convent, Cabra.
Cardinal Van Roey, Archbishop of Mechlin, stayed at Shrewsbury Road, Dublin, as the guest of the Belgian Consul-General, M. Goor.
Cardinal Hlond, Primate of Poland, stayed at Loreto Abbey, Rathfarnham.

Two of the Cardinals chose to stay on the 'floating hotels' in which they had travelled. (*Courtesy of Niall Dardis, Dublin Port Archives.*)

Cardinal Dougherty, Archbishop of Philadelphia, stayed aboard the SS *Lapland*, in which he travelled to Ireland.

Cardinal Hayes, Archbishop of New York, was a guest of F.A. Sterling, United States Minister, at the American Embassy.

Cardinal O'Connell, Archbishop of Boston, stayed aboard the *Samaria*, in which he travelled to Ireland.

Congressus Dublinensis

On 22 June, the solemn inauguration of the Congress took place in the Pro-Cathedral. The Cathedral, which was beautifully decorated with hanging baskets of flowers and great papal banners on either side of the nave, was packed to capacity with prelates and dignitaries. As the Legate entered the Palestrina choir again sang 'Ecce Sacerdos Magnus'. As the Legate knelt in front of the altar the entire congregation sang 'Veni Creator'. Monsignor Spellman then read a letter from Pope Pius expressing his wish for a successful Congress and the cherishing of the Holy Eucharist. Archbishop Byrne made an address and called upon the Bishop of Namur, on behalf of the Permanent Committee of the International Eucharistic Congress, to formally inaugurate the Congress. No doubt to the delight of the congregation and to the vast crowds listening to the Mass outside, the Bishop stated that given the sights already witnessed, the Dublin Congress 'promises, in numbers, devotion and splendour to stand comparison with the most glorious that have ever been celebrated'. There followed an address by the Papal Legate who, on conclusion, gave Solemn Benediction of the Blessed Sacrament.

Later that night, amid spectacular lighting displays, and with the words 'Adoramus, Laudamus, Glorificamus' beamed into the night sky in gigantic 'letters of light', midnight Mass was held in all churches to mark the opening night of the Congress, with many churches simply unable to accommodate all of those gathering for Mass. The celebrants were mostly Cardinals, or archbishops or bishops. In virtually every household a candle was lit in a window through the night. The great buildings of the city were lavishly floodlit. Out in Dublin Bay the large ships used their searchlights to light up all the smaller craft. The city was ablaze with light.

Mass Meeting of Men

Although large crowds of people attended Masses in various Dublin churches throughout the week, the greatest indicator of religious fervour was the massive number of people who participated in the main Congress events. The first of these, the Mass Meeting of Men (not an actual Mass), held in the 'Fifteen Acres' of the Phoenix Park on Thursday 23 June in front of a giant altar flanked by colonnades, was witnessed by a congregation of approximately 250,000 people.

At 8p.m. on another beautiful summer evening the Papal Legate moved from the Hibernian School (adjacent to the altar and the buildings were used as robing rooms) to take his seat on the throne at the High Altar. The first address, 'An tAifreann Laetheamhail' was given in Irish by the Bishop of Raphoe. This was followed by an address in English, 'The Blessed Eucharist,

Procession leaving the Pro-Cathedral after the Solemn Opening of the Congress. (*Courtesy of Dublin Diocesan Archives, Eucharistic Congress Collection.*)

Glorificamus – this 'sky-writing' was part of the lighting display on the opening night of the Congress. (*Courtesy of Dublin Diocesan Archives.*)

Lighting display on O'Connell Street. (*Courtesy of Dublin Diocesan Archives, Eucharistic Congress Collection.*)

Midnight Mass at St Joseph's church, Berkeley Road. As the attendances were so large at these Masses in the city-centre churches, often any available priest would have to say Mass outside for those who could not gain admission. (*Courtesy of Dublin Diocesan Archives.*)

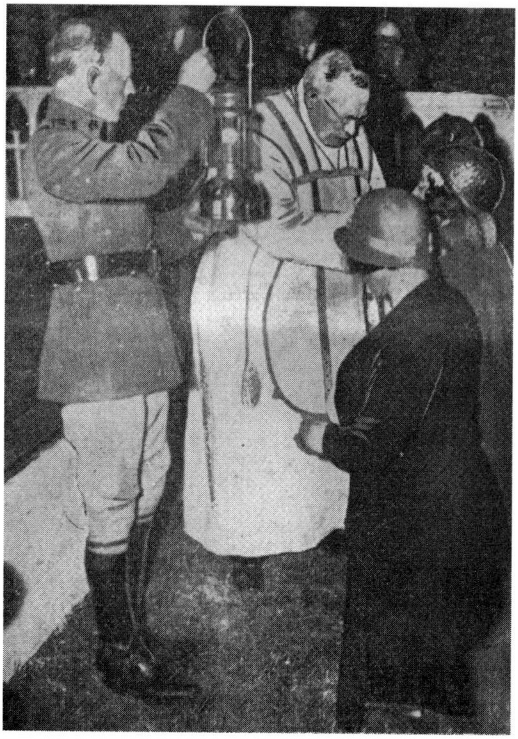

The Archbishop of St Andrew and Edinburgh, Revd Dr MacDonald offering communion, with an army officer holding a lamp at the Midnight Mass at the Artane Camp where a very large congregation gathered for Mass. (*Courtesy of Dublin Diocesan Archives, Eucharistic Congress Collection.*)

A view of the congregation at the Mass Meeting of Men. The Papal Legate is seen proceeding towards the altar. (*Courtesy of Dublin Diocesan Archives.*)

the Sacrament of Charity and Peace', given by the Archbishop of St Louis, Revd Dr Glennon. Hymns were then sung in Irish, Latin and English. This was followed by an address by the Legate who mentioned his joyful experiences thus far in Dublin:

> Although my expectations on coming here were very high, and I had prepared myself to witness something that was extraordinary, I am obliged to say that in all truth what has occurred is far beyond anything I could have conceived as possible. I have been inspired and edified to an extent which is beyond the power of words to describe, and I know that God in His goodness will bless you all most abundantly for this wonderful tribute of love and of devotion and of fidelity which you have given.
>
> I wish I could tell you how overjoyed I am to be here and at all the things I have seen. Never, never can I forget them, and you my dear men, must never forget them either. Nor do I think that you can forget them, and neither will God forget these things…

At the conclusion of the Legate's address an instruction was given to the congregation to light and hold aloft their candles (which on careful instruction they had all brought with them). Benediction was given by the Legate as the candles remained burning; the magnificent sea of light thus created was marvelled at by the journalists present.

***

The Great Altar

The following passage is from Canon Boylan's *The Book of the Congress* (English & Co.: Wexford, 1934), p. 109:

> The Congress altar stood on a substructure of two rows of ten steps each with a platform between the two rows of steps. The width of the platform at the top of the steps was 43½ feet. The whole platform on which the altar rested ten feet above the ground, and the altar itself stood 2½ feet above that level, so that the predella was 12½ feet above ground-level. The table of the altar was 16 feet above ground level.
>
> The baldachino, standing on the platform at the top of the steps, consisted of a circular dome supported on four graceful Ionic columns erected on pedestals, and the entablature were ornamented. The front of the entablature curved to correspond with the curve of the dome. The drum of the dome was decorated with a guilloche ornament surmounted with acanthus leaves. The surface of the dome proper was ribbed and panelled: the dome supported a cupola which was covered by a smaller dome – the whole being surmounted by a cross.
>
> Drapery was hung at the front and sides of the altar, and at the back of the altar there was a solid partition curved in sympathy with the entablature and the dome. The sides of the altar were enclosed with glass. The structure generally consisted of a strong steel framework, and all the ornamentation was done in fibrous plaster. The dominating colours were white and gold.

An aerial view of the altar and colonnades in the Phoenix Park. The Hibernian School buildings seen in the background were used for vesting. The open fields of Ballyfermot are seen in the distance. (*O'Reilly Collection.*)

The altar in the Phoenix Park was designed by the 'Congress Architect' John J. Robinson, one of the foremost church architects in Ireland at the time. He later received an Honorary Master's Degree for his services. The dome and curving colonnades are reminiscent of St Peter's in Rome. The universal architecture of classicism was here intended to celebrate the universality of the Catholic Church, as specified in the commission. (*Courtesy of Dublin Diocesan Archives, Eucharistic Congress Collection.*)

The height from the top of the cross to the ground was 70½ feet; the entablature was 27 feet above the platform and between the pedestals of the pillars on the front and sides there was a space of 15½ feet.

On each side of the altar but separated from it somewhat was a covered colonnade extending in a graceful sweep with the extremes turning towards the people: each extreme ended in a pavilion bearing a small dome in harmony with the dome over the altar. The covered colonnades were filled with seats for visiting prelates.

Places were set for the cardinals under two thrones of crimson velvet at each side of the altar. At the gospel corner was set the Cardinal Legate's throne, and close by his throne were seats for the pontifical mission.

There was an entrance door from behind at each side of the altar for the use of the ceremonialists. The altar stood with its back to the Hibernian School, and facing across the broad expanse of the 'Fifteen Acres'.

***

Archbishop of St Louis, Revd Dr Glennon. (*Courtesy of Dublin Diocesan Archives, Eucharistic Congress Collection.*)

Archbishop Glennon

The Archbishop of Saint Louis, John J. Glennon was born in Co. Meath and studied for the priesthood at All Hallows College in Dublin. When he was appointed Archbishop of Saint Louis in 1902 he became the youngest archbishop in the world (aged forty). In 1945 he was named a Cardinal by Pope Pius XII. Travelling to Ireland after the completion of the ceremonies in Rome, he became very ill and died while staying with President Seán T. O'Kelly in Arás an Uachtaráin. A remarkably large funeral followed in Dublin before his body was returned to St Louis and buried in the Cathedral Basilica of St Louis.

***

The Mass Meeting of Women in the park on 24 June was attended by some 200,000 women. The programme of the ceremony was very similar to the previous night, with the Papal Legate again presiding. The first address was given in Irish, 'Cuarta ar an tSacraimint Ró-Naomhtha' by the Bishop of Down and Connor. The next address 'The Work of Women in Modern Catholic Life' was given by the Archbishop of St Andrew's and Edinburgh, Revd Dr MacDonald. Hymns were sung in Irish, Latin and English. The Legate then addressed the gathering. Candles were again lit for Benediction, but on this occasion (the only time during the entire Congress celebrations) rain fell and the ceremony was somewhat marred.

Chesterton on the Weather

As the Congress week drew to an end, the patch of glowing weather which had been stretched like a golden canopy, strangely and almost insecurely, began to show signs of strain or schism. There was a hint of storm in the still heat, and here and there random splashes of rain. It was naturally a topic of anxious talk, and it gave birth to one great saying, which I shall always remember as one of those tremendous oracles that sometimes come from the innocent. A priest told me that he had heard a very poor threadbare working woman saying in a tram, with a resignation perhaps slightly touched with tartness: 'Well, if it rains now, He'll have brought it on Himself.'

(*Christendom in Dublin*, p.59.)

***

Crowds of women trying to get on board a packed tram from O'Connell Bridge in the direction of the Phoenix Park for the Mass Meeting of Women. The tram service was in phenomenal demand during the Congress, particularly this route from the city centre towards the Park. It was later estimated that approximately 4 million passengers travelled on the tram service during the Congress period. (*Courtesy of National Library of Ireland.*)

The Mass Meeting of Women at the Phoenix Park. (*Courtesy of Dublin Diocesan Archives, Eucharistic Congress Collection.*)

Children's Mass

The Children's Mass at noon on Saturday 25 June, saw approximately 100,000 children gather in the park. The occasion was graced with glorious weather and the children were mostly dressed in white, with many of the girls wearing wreaths and veils. The Mass was celebrated by the Archbishop of Sydney, Revd Dr Kelly. The music of the Mass was sung beautifully by a specially trained choir of 2,700 children drawn from primary and secondary schools of the Archdiocese of Dublin. At the conclusion of the Mass the Legate addressed the children referring to them as the pride and boast of the Catholic Church and called on them to receive Holy Communion frequently:

> I exhort you to receive Our Lord always with the proper disposition – that is, with a careful and devout preparation to be followed by a fervent and devout thanksgiving and with Jesus in your hearts learn to speak to him and to harken to His voice. Pray to him for yourselves, for your parents, for your relatives and friends, and pray also for your beloved country that the Lord will always bless and keep its people good and holy.

As the Cardinal Legate left he was cheered continuously while being driven on a circuit around the congregation of children.

Convent National School, Townsend Street group at the Children's Mass. Teachers, stewards and a Girl Guide (far right) are seen amongst the children. (*Courtesy of Dublin Diocesan Archives, Eucharistic Congress Collection.*)

Scout offering a cup of water (garnished from the special water supply to the 'Fifteen Acres') to a girl at the Children's Mass. All of the girls are dressed in white and wearing veils. They are not necessarily a Communion group as most girls at the Mass would have been dressed similarly. (*Courtesy of National Library of Ireland.*)

The Papal Legate being driven among the congregation following the Children's Mass. (*Courtesy of Dublin Diocesan Archives, Eucharistic Congress Collection.*)

Solemn Pontifical Mass, Phoenix Park

The main Pontifical High Mass on 26 June was attended by an estimated one million people. The great open space in front of the altar had been divided up into sections and sub-sections marked by letters and numbers. These sections and subsections had been assigned to particular groups – countries, diocese, parishes, confraternities, etc. Such information had been published in newspapers, advance programmes, etc., well in advance of the event. Stewards, Boy Scouts and Civic Guards were everywhere at hand in the park to ensure people arrived at their appropriate locations. As one commentator reported, 'The "Fifteen Acres" was like a great city in outline, with streets and squares and (in a fashion) residences, and business centres, and all of these were as well defined, and as easy to identify, as the districts of a modern city.'

At 12.45p.m. the first procession (of the Monsignori) to the High Altar took place. They were followed by the Bishops, the Archbishops, the Cardinals (with train-bearers and gentlemen-in-waiting) and culminating with the Papal Legate (with his brilliantly uniformed Chamberlains). It was a very impressive spectacle on yet another glorious summer day. On a platform at the base of the Altar a guard of honour saluted the Legate. Six trumpeters were posted adjacent to them. Tense moments followed as it was anticipated that the Pope's message would be delivered just before the Mass was to begin, but no message was forthcoming. When it was realised that Pope Pius would not speak for some time, the Mass began. The celebrant of the Mass was the Archbishop of Baltimore, Michael Curley, a native of Athlone. The music of the Mass was Palestrina's *Missa Brevis*, which was beautifully rendered by the choir of 2,000 led by Vincent O'Brien. Before the Credo, the Cardinal Legate addressed the large congregation, passionately extolling reverence for the Eucharist.

Crowds on the Main Avenue in the Phoenix Park making their way to the Pontifical High Mass. (*Courtesy of National Library of Ireland.*)

Aerial view of the congregation gathering for High Mass. (*O'Reilly Collection.*)

Following the Credo, John McCormack (a former student of O'Brien's) sang the offertory motet 'Panis Angelicus' to a captivated audience. McCormack, a Papal Count since 1928 and wearing the distinctive robes, was an internationally renowned tenor whose greatly valued and emotionally significant participation confirmed the collective desire for a professional approach to the Congress and added to the sense of pride that so many people derived from the event. It was an unforgettable moment for all present. By all accounts McCormack never sang more soulfully and or with more beauty of tone. His performance was world class and, vitally, it was an Irish performance. With a gregarious and cheerful personality and attending so many of the other Congress ceremonies and functions, McCormack was a truly excellent ambassador for Ireland and this was widely appreciated.

***

'Panis Angelicus' ('Bread of Angels')

Panis Angelicus fit panis hominum;
Dat panis coelicus figures terminum:
O res mirabilus! Manducat Dominum.
(pauper, pauper, servus et humilis.)

State dignitaries (including various TDs, the Lord Mayor and the Ceann Comhairle) at prayer, High Mass, Phoenix Park. (*Courtesy of the Dublin Diocesan Archives, Eucharistic Congress Collection.*)

Te Trina Deitas, unique poscimus,
Sic nos tu visita, sicut te colimus;
Per tuas semitas duc nos quo tendimus,
(Ad lucem quam inhabitas.)

The words of 'Panis Angelicus' come from a hymn 'Sacris Solemnis' written by Thomas Aquinas in the thirteenth century for the Feast of Corpus Christi. This particular verse (properly strophe) was set to music most famously by Cesar Franck in 1872. It was Franck's romantic adaptation which was performed in the Phoenix Park.

***

John McCormack

Letter from John McCormack to Archbishop Byrne, 18 September 1931:

My dear Archbishop,

May I offer to your Grace my services during the Eucharistic Congress, whether as a Papal Chamberlain or in my more familiar role of singer.

On the 8th of the month we had a wonderful Pontifical High Mass celebrated by the Apostolic Delegate in the giant Coliseum here in Los Angeles. The occasion was the 150th anniversary of the founding of the city. More than 120,000 people were assembled. I was specially privileged by being invited to sing at the offertory of the Holy Mass, and there, before the mightiest audience of my long career and under the most inspiring and inspiriting circumstances, I sang 'Panis Angelicus' by the great Catholic composer, Cesar Franck.

It would be a great honour and I would deem it a privilege to sing the 'Panis Angelicus' during the opening High Mass of the Congress and to offer my services to your Grace is this object of this letter. My debt of gratitude to Dublin is too great to ever be repaid [Apart from having received his early training in Dublin, McCormack was conferred a Freeman of Dublin in 1923], but I would be proud to help next year, and at the same time make public demonstration of that faith, for which I ever thank God.

With most respectful affectionate greetings to your Grace, in which Countess McCormack joins me.

Believe me,
Your Grace's most affectionate servant,
John, Count McCormack

***

John McCormack.

Archbishop of Baltimore, Revd Dr Curley (*Courtesy of Dublin Diocesan Archives.*)

Archbishop Curley

The Archbishop of Baltimore, Michael Curley, the celebrant of the Mass, was a former school friend of John McCormack at the Marist Brother's College in Athlone. Curley later went on to attend the Urban College of the Propaganda Fide in Rome (another former student of Cardinal Lauri, like Archbishop Byrne). After becoming a bishop in the United States in 1914, Curley wrote to his mother in Athlone, 'I leave it to you to bring it home to your people that their place is at home with their shoulders to the wheel to give us a greater and better Ireland. This is the message I want to leave you, not that I love America less, but because I love Ireland more.' It was a source of great pride to Curley to have been chosen by Cardinal Lauri to celebrate the High Mass in the Phoenix Park. As most of the vast throng in the Park were aware due to the wide media coverage, it was a particularly poignant choice as Curley's ninety-two-year-old mother was gravely ill in Athlone. In the Ireland of the time no mother could have had a greater honour bestowed upon one of her sons.

Following the motet, the consecration was heralded with a command in Irish to the attendant guard of officers to present arms, and, in a brilliantly orchestrated sequence, thirty-six glinting

Archbishop Curley (centre) with John McCormack (left) and Seán MacEoin (right). (*Courtesy of Gearóid O'Brien.*)

sword blades were pointed to the altar. The total silence among the congregation was broken by six trumpeters who sounded a general salute. This was followed by the tolling of an ancient bell traditionally associated with St Patrick (removed from the National Museum especially for the Mass). From the consecration to the communion, the guard of honour continued with swords dramatically rendered ('tiolalaigh claoite') in a highly impressive gesture of reverence. All sequences were performed exquisitely.

Eoin O'Duffy

Eoin O'Duffy, Commissioner of the Garda Síochána, was the Chief Marshall at all the ceremonies in the Phoenix Park, as well as Chairman of the Stewarding Sub-Committee (whose meetings he often failed to attend). O'Duffy had also served as Marshall during the Catholic Emancipation Centenary Celebrations in 1929 and he clearly relished in his role at the Congress. However, O'Duffy was always distrusted by the head of Government, Éamon de Valera, and was eventually dismissed from his post in February 1933. His career and prospects (once so promising) went rapidly downhill, eventually descending into fiasco. He apparently later boasted to General Franco (when he joined Franco's forces in 1936) that he had once 'commanded' a million people in Ireland. The General was less impressed on discovering the full detail.

Chesterton on St Patrick's Bell

> At one of the moments when Catholics would be accustomed to hear the clear and rather shrill tinkle of the bell of the 'Santus', there were was heard a sound that was almost unique in human history. It was as faint as the sound of a far-off sheep-bell and as weak as the bleat of a sheep; but there was something on it that was not only weighty, but curiously hard; almost dead; without the resonance that we mean by music. It was as if it came out of the Stone Age; when even musical instruments might be made of stone. It was the bell of St Patrick, which had been silent for 1,500 years.
>
> I know of no poetical parallel to the effect of that little noise in that huge presence. From far away in the most forgotten of the centuries, as if down avenues that were colonnades of corpses, one dead man had spoken. It was St Patrick; and he only said: 'My Master is here.'
>
> And after that, I for one could realise little but a catastrophic silence, till it could be crowned with the only fitting close. From the four corners of the sacred enclosure the all-shattering trumpets shouted, like the Sons of God shouting for joy. And all along the front there ran, like a sudden lightening, the light upon the lifted swords; for all soldiers standing before the altar saluted with a blazing salute of steel, carrying the hilt to the head in the old swordsman's salutation, and then striking outwards, in the ancient gesture of the Romans.
>
> 'Her face was like a King's Command
> When all the swords are drawn.'

(*Christendom in Dublin* pp53–55.)

Eoin O'Duffy, Chief Marshall for the Congress. (*Courtesy of Dublin Diocesan Archives, Eucharistic Congress Collection.*)

'St Patrick's Bell' (*Courtesy of Dublin Diocesan Archives, Eucharistic Congress Collection.*)

Message from Pope Pius XI

Just before the blessing a voice was heard from the Vatican, 'Attendite! Beatissimus Pater statim loquetur vobis.' (Attention! The Holy Father is about to address you!) The Pope's voice was then heard across the airwaves:

> In the Name of the Father and of the Son, and of the Holy Ghost. Amen. Behold I am with you, my most dear children in Christ! We are with you, in the first place, as a Father with his children on their day of rejoicing, so that we may have a share in your joy, and in the triumph of the Eucharist.
>
> We are with you, further, to join with you in supplication to God, Almighty and Merciful, that, moved by the prayers of his Church, He may, in the present great tribulation of all peoples, graciously bestow the gifts of unity and peace which are symbolised in the Eucharistic offering.
>
> Finally with heart and lips, as your Father, We wish you joy, and we impart with the most special affection Our apostolic Benediction. May then, through the intercession and merits of Blessed Mary, ever virgin, the Queen of Ireland, of Blessed Michael the archangel, of blessed John the Baptist, of the blessed apostles Peter and Paul, of the Blessed patriarch, Patrick, of the blessed saints of Ireland, and of all the saints, the blessing of God Almighty, Father, Son and Holy Ghost, descend upon you and upon Ireland so dear to us and to you; and remain with you always! [Translation from Latin.]

Pope Pius XI broadcasting a live message from the Vatican to the Phoenix Park. (*Courtesy of Dublin Diocesan Archives, Eucharistic Congress Collection.*)

Amplifier beside the altar in the Phoenix Park. (*Courtesy of Dublin Diocesan Archives, Eucharistic Congress Collection.*)

Public Address System

The Public Address System which was installed in Dublin for the Congress was the largest and the most ambitious system ever installed anywhere in the world. Some 500 loudspeakers were in place, covering not only the great congregational area in the Phoenix Park but also more than fifteen miles of streets. Dublin became a virtual open-air Cathedral, as the entire Mass was broadcast to many throughout the city who, it was noted, could be seen giving all the necessary responses. The street loudspeakers were operated by ten different amplifying stations distributed along the processional routes. Each loudspeaker had a range, in calm conditions, of half a mile. Without loudspeakers it would have been impossible to synchronise the singing of such a large congregation as gathered in the Phoenix Park. Nineteen microphone points were arranged on or around the High Altar; six for the men's choir, six for the children's choir, four for the organ and soloist's positions, and three on the various parts of the Altar itself. The loudspeakers in the park were used with excellent effect at the conclusion of the service for marshalling the enormous crowds into orderly processions. A vast and complex backup system was also in place in case of any problems.

The use of the street system was not limited solely to the broadcasting of services and music from the Congress altar and from the Pro-Cathedral. At 10a.m. on each morning of the Congress week, the programme of the day's events was announced all over the street system from the Dublin studio. The internationalism of the event (and the sheer confidence of the organisers) was reflected in the fact that these announcements were regularly given out in six different languages and interpreters were employed specially for the event.

The entire Mass was organised with great precision and detail. Approximately 20,000 stewards (all voluntary) and 4,000 Catholic Boy Scouts, all with detailed instructions and duties, offered their services for the occasion – as they had throughout the Congress period. Large catering tents had been erected, information bureaus were provided, first-aid stations, toilets – even a special water supply to the 'Fifteen Acres' was established for the occasion.

Procession of the Blessed Sacrament to O'Connell Bridge

After an interval of half an hour for refreshment, the Mass was followed by a procession of the Blessed Sacrament (a central part of every Eucharistic Congress), involving most of the enormous congregation, from the park to the city centre. The Blessed Sacrament was carried on a sort of movable dais or throne – a platform borne on four wheels on which stood a support for the Monstrance and a kneeler and chair for the Cardinal Legate. A select number of distinguished laymen were appointed as Canopy Bearers: President de Valera; Seán T. O'Kelly, Vice-President; the Speaker of the Dáil, the Chief Justice, William Cosgrave, TD; Senator Farren, the Chairman of the Senate; the Lord Mayors of Dublin and Cork; the Mayors of Limerick, Kilkenny, Waterford, Clonmel, Drogheda, Wexford and Sligo; Joseph Devlin, MP; Cahir Healy, MP; Senator T.J. Campbell, KC; Dr D. Coffey, President, University College Dublin; Count John McCormack; T. McLoughlin; J.J. Shiel, and Sir Joseph Glynn. As the pictures indicate, the Canopy Bearers, however important their role was symbolically, were merely holding cords. The dais was drawn by eight young priests who can be seen closest to the canopy on both sides.

Detail of the Procession

The procession was arranged to move in four columns of eight abreast of men, and four of eight abreast of women. The units were carefully determined well in advance and the various subdivisions and divisions in the 'Fifteen Acres' knew or could readily ascertain the column with which it was

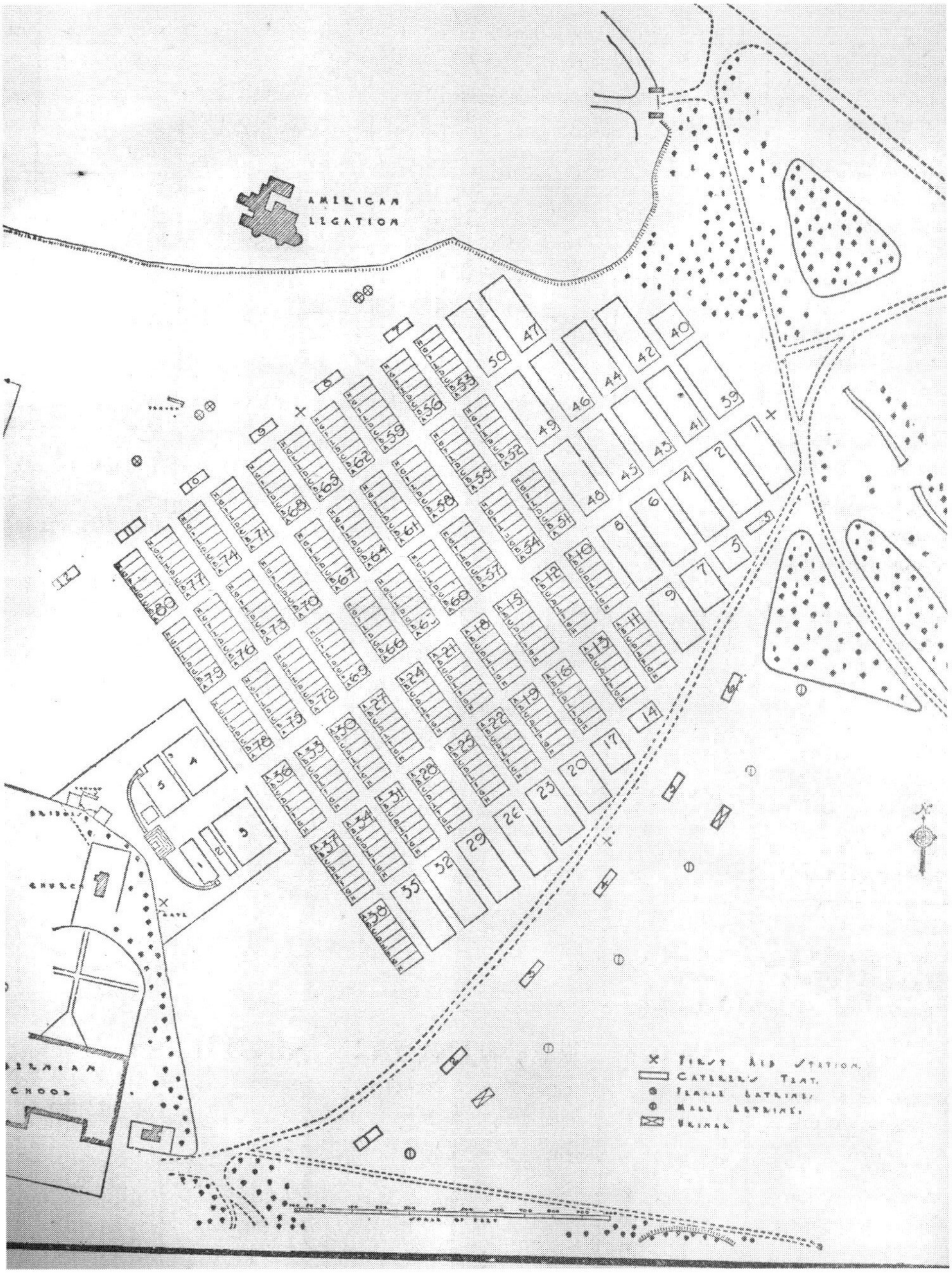

Map showing the arrangement of the congregation in the 'Fifteen Acres' of the Phoenix Park. This map was featured in most Irish newspapers in advance of the Congress, followed by a number of pages outlining in detail where the various diocesan and even parochial groups would be located. For instance, men from the Cork City parishes were to be located in Section 33, subsections A, B, C and D. The women of Cork City would be located in Section 76, subsections A, B and C. Those from other parts of the diocese of Cork would be located close by, as would those from the neighbouring diocese of Cloyne. (*Courtesy of Dublin Diocesan Archives, Eucharistic Congress Collection.*)

expected to march. The columns were headed in each case by a troop of cavalry of the Army in official uniform, and the routes along which the columns were to march were held open by cordons of soldiers. Between the cavalry at the head of each column and the people an officer of the Garda Síochána marched to set the pace for the column. The first column of men left the park by the Island Bridge Gate, and marched along Conyngham Road, and Parkgate Street to Kingsbridge. Crossing Kingsbridge, the column (always marching on the right side of the road) marched by Stevens' Lane, James' Street, Thomas Street, Lamb's Alley, Back Lane, John Dillon Street, Nicholas Street, Christchurch Place, Lord Edward Street, Dame Street, College Green, College Street, Townsend Street, and Tara Street, to Burgh Quay.

The second column of men marched along the right side of the Main Road of the park to Parkgate Street, where they marched along the centre of the road. Their route then passed along the Northern Quays, crossed the Liffey at Watling Street Bridge, went through Watling Street, Thomas Street, Cornmarket, High Street, Christchurch Place, Lord Edward Street, Dame Street, College Green and Westmoreland Street. This column then occupied D'Olier Street, and College Street as its final position.

A third column of men marched along the left side of the main road of the park to Parkgate Street, and then marched by Barrack Street, Blackhall Place, Ellis Quay, Northern Quays, Capel Street, Parnell Street, to the Parnell Monument and the right side of O'Connell Street. When the

The beginning of the Procession of the Blessed Sacrament with a Guard of Honour on either side. W.T. Cosgrave can be seen to the left of the Canopy. Éamon de Valera (obscured from view in this picture) is walking parallel with him on the other side of the Canopy. (*Courtesy of Dublin Diocesan Archives, Eucharistic Congress Collection.*)

The main processional route from the park onto Parkgate Street. (*O'Reilly Collection.*)

right side of O'Connell Street was fully occupied, the remainder of this column marched along the right side of Parnell Street and Middle and Lower Gardiner Street to Beresford Place, halting finally at allotted positions near the Custom House.

A fourth column of men crossed the Main Road of the Park to the Zoo Road, and thence to the North Circular Road Gate: from there it marched by the North Circular Road, Berkeley Street, North Frederick Street, Rotunda, to O'Connell Street (left side). When the left side of O'Connell Street was fully occupied, the rest of the column moved along the left side of Parnell Street, and Lower and Middle Gardiner Street to Beresford Place, and took up their allotted positions at the Custom House. Behind each of the four columns of men marched a column of women.

Canon Boylan, *The Book of the Congress*, pp191–192.

***

Order of Procession

Cavalry
Banner of the Blessed Sacrament
Men (four files of eight)
Cross bearer and acolytes
Revd Brothers (two files of eight)
First portion of Choir
Clergy in order of preferences (two files of eight)
Priests' Choir
Canons of Metropolitan Chapter (one file of eight)
Torch bearers
Thurifers
Military Guard
Blessed Sacrament
Canopy Bearers
Cardinals and their Suites (single file)
Archbishops (one file of two)
Bishops (one file of two)
Other prelates (one file of four)
Ministers (one file of four)
Second portion of Choir

Other Distinguished and representative persons, in the following order:
Dáil
Senate
Representative persons from the six Northern Counties
Bearers of Papal titles
Foreign Consuls
Dublin Corporation and Corporation of Coastal Burrough
(The above in one file of eight)
Corporations
County Councils
Harbour Boards
Vocational Councils
Urban District Councils
Boards of Public Assistance
Others
(The above in two files of eight)
Distinguished and representative Women
(Two files of eight)
Special group of Female Singers
Women
(Two files of eight)

The Canopy in the Procession moving along the city quays with another relay of Canopy Bearers. John McCormack, in the splendid uniform of a Papal Count, can be seen towards the right. (*Courtesy of Dublin Diocesan Archives, Eucharistic Congress Collection.*)

***

Chesterton on 'General Will'

If we take all current statements about the gradual decay of all dogmas of Christianity, we shall find that they are pretty roughly true, if we apply them to the dogmas of Democracy. The commonest form of denial, especially among the most cultivated and capable critics, is the denial of that dogma of Rousseau, which is called 'the General Will'. The Humanists of America, the Fascists of Italy, even the Bolshevists of Russia, all the most recent schools that have revolutionised the old revolutionary tradition, all dismiss this democratic mystery as a myth. There is no such thing as a General Will. How could there be a General Will?

Now it is quite certain that a General Will walked about the streets of Dublin for a week. It is quite certain that there was practical harmony, because there was theoretical unity. There was truly and actually, in the threadbare and vulgarised phrase of the politicians, a Will of the People; and it did prevail. The order was not only organisation. It is true that the organisation was very good.

> Anybody who shall say henceforth that the Irish cannot organise, or cannot rule, or are not practical enough for practical politics, will certainly have the laugh against him forever. There has never been a modern mass meeting, of anything like this size, that passed off so smoothly, or with so few miscalculations or misfortunes. But nobody who looked at the crowd could for one instant mistake its order for organisation. The mob could be managed successfully, because every man in the mob passionately wished the ceremony to be a success. There were men of many minds on many other matters, including politics, but on this they were of one mind; that is, they had a General Will. That mob, alone among modern societies, had self-government. It really had self-government, in the old sense of self-control. If it had not been organised, it would have organised itself. It was a vision very extraordinary, to any man who has seen the bewildering facts of modern politics, and compared them with monotonous repetition of modern abstractions. It was Self-Determination of the People.

(*Christendom in Dublin*, pp 43–44.)

***

As the sun shone brilliantly on the Liffey from the West, the Blessed Sacrament approached the altar at O'Connell Bridge. As the Papal Legate arrived at the altar he was vested in a cope which had been made especially for him by the weavers of Dublin. With perhaps a sense of a truly historic occasion coming to an end, and an awareness of their essential part in that occasion, the Benediction hymns were sung with great fervour by the massive congregation. At the blessing, the trumpeters sounded the general salute and the guard of honour saluted with their swords. After the Benediction, the Legate addressed the congregation, 'This magnificent Eucharistic Congress is now being concluded. For yet a little while I shall remain in your midst, and then I shall return to the Holy Father, to tell of this wondrous event, the triumph of our Lord in the Blessed Sacrament, which you have made one of the most notable occurrences of His Glorious Pontificate...'

After the Legate concluded his address, the congregation sang two popular hymns ('Faith of our Fathers' and 'God Bless Our Pope') and even after the general dispersal was sounded many continued cheering and singing into the night.

After the Congress

The day after the official Congress events came to a close in Dublin the Papal Legate was conferred a Freeman of Dublin in a moving ceremony in the Mansion House. Cardinal Lauri's cheerful countenance, courtesy, and gracious personality, along with his dignified bearing and impressive oratory (speaking very good English and even attempting to speak Irish), had made a very positive impression. Some Irish clerics were already acquainted with him long before the Congress. The Archbishop of Dublin, Edward Byrne, was one of those who studied under Cardinal Lauri when he lectured at the esteemed Propaganda Fide (Propagation of the Faith) University in Rome many years previously. Lauri was a very distinguished ecclesiastic who, having served for many years as papal nuncio to Peru and then Poland, was raised to Cardinal

An aerial view of the final Benediction at O'Connell Bridge. (*Courtesy of Dublin Diocesan Archives, Eucharistic Congress Collection.*)

in 1926 and became a special advisor to Pius XI before becoming the Holy Father's 'grand penitentiary' in 1932.

During his final week in Ireland, the Cardinal Legate visited a number of Irish towns, where the welcome he received was just as jubilant as it had been in Dublin. On 28 June, he visited the Primate of All-Ireland, Cardinal Joseph MacRory at Armagh, where an address of welcome was presented to the Legate on behalf of the Armagh Urban Council. In villages as well as in towns *en route* (overwhelmingly Catholic) throngs of people welcomed him. There were highly impressive scenes in Balbriggan, Drogheda, Dundalk and Newry churches, where special welcomes were also given. On the following day the Legate paid an informal visit to St Patrick's College Maynooth, where he was received by the president of the college and members of the college staff. On 30 June, the Legate and his suite journeyed to Killarney by special train and enjoyed very enthusiastic receptions at Thurles (where he was welcomed by the Archbishop of Cashel among many others), Mallow (where an address was presented to him by the Urban Council) and Killarney. Following an address of welcome in Killarney and a great procession from the train station to the Cathedral, the Legate was accompanied by the Bishop of Kerry on a tour of some of the famous local beauty spots. As on so many other occasions, visiting journalists noted the beautiful decorations in the streets and local

A ceremony in the Round Room of the Mansion House during which the Legate (centre) was conferred an honorary Freeman of Dublin. John McCormack can be seen singing on the left beside the piano. During the ceremony he sang a hymn to 'Christ the King' and a popular Irish ballad 'Come back to Erin', once again making an excellent impression on his audience. (*O'Reilly Collection.*)

countryside. The Cardinal Legate remained in Killarney that night and on the following morning celebrated Mass in the Cathedral. In the afternoon he returned to Dublin by special train. More scenes of tumultuous enthusiasm were witnessed in Maryborough (Port Laoise) on the return journey to Dublin as the Legate received another address of welcome. Clearly moved by the reception he had received throughout his visit he met with all members of the organising committees and sub-committees of the Congress at Holy Cross College, Clonliffe, on the following day and congratulated them on their excellent work and expressed his conviction (and that of all Irish people who participated) that this Congress had surpassed all others.

On his departure from Ireland early the next morning (3 July), the Legate wrote to the Archbishop of Dublin:

> I shall never forget the unforgettably glorious days of this Eucharistic Congress … all have participated, all have co-operated to make this Congress a triumph, government and civic leaders, as well as ecclesiastical authorities, priests members of religious communities, men, women and children, have all united to make this Eucharistic Congress a plebiscite of love for the Blessed Eucharist, a plebiscite of devotion to the vicar of Christ.

The Papal Legate after visiting the Oliver Plunkett Memorial Church in Drogheda on his way to Armagh. (*O'Reilly Collection.*)

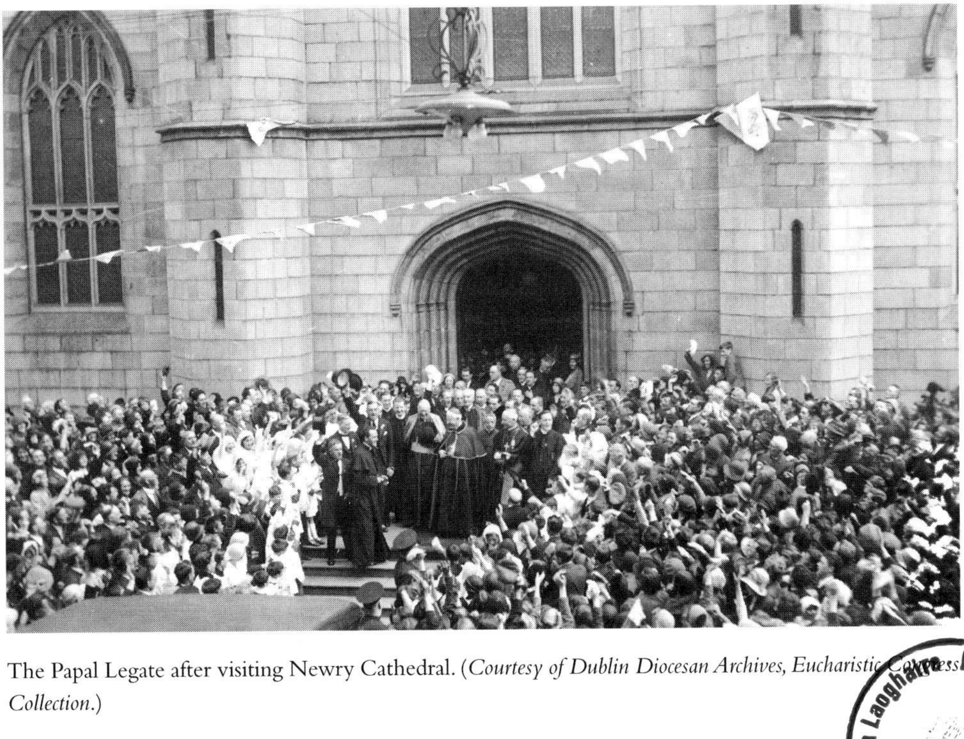

The Papal Legate after visiting Newry Cathedral. (*Courtesy of Dublin Diocesan Archives, Eucharistic Congress Collection.*)

The special train for the Papal Legate's journey to Killarney. The luxurious carriage in which he travelled had been made especially for King Edward VII's visit to Ireland in 1903. The royal saloons included a beautifully equipped dining saloon. The engine was decorated and bore the papal crest. The driver and fireman wore rosettes and cap bands of Papal colours. (*Courtesy of Dublin Diocesan Archives, Eucharistic Congress Collection.*)

The Papal Legate received in Killarney. (*Courtesy of Dublin Diocesan Archives, Eucharistic Congress Collection.*)

T R A N S L A T I O N

University Hall,
DUBLIN.

Dear Mr. O'Reilly,

I do not wish to leave Dublin without expressing my admiration for the perfect preparation made for our 31st Congress; it has never been done so well and it will never be excelled !

I am going away not only marvelling and edified but also sanctified !

Ireland has shown to the world how God should be loved, even to giving one's life for him, and I am confident that when each pilgrim to the Congress goes home he will endeavour to profit by the example which has been shown at Dublin.

Please give my most respectful greetings to Mrs. O'Reilly and receive for yourself until I shall be able to call you "my dear colleague" my warmest regards.

Yours sincerely,

COMTE HENRI d'YANVILLE.

Translation of a letter from Comte Henri d'Yanville, a member of the Permanent Committee of Eucharistic Congresses, to Frank O'Reilly. (*O'Reilly Collection*.)

Expositio

The Congress presents a very valuable snapshot of a period in modern Irish history when levels of Catholic devotion were at a remarkably high point. This was a time when it was extremely common for young men and women to join sodality or confraternity groups. Some confraternities were very large – the Archconfraternity of the Sacred Heart in Phibsborough had approximately 4,000 members. Parish missions were extremely well attended in this period. The retreat movement was also very strong. Thousands of Dubliners went on retreats (often over a weekend) at Rathfarnham Castle, Milltown Park, and other popular retreat houses. There was a very vibrant Catholic press, with numerous popular religious periodicals in circulation. The *Irish Messenger of the Sacred Heart* had over 250,000 subscribers. The Catholic Truth Society of Ireland (with whom Frank O'Reilly worked) published many popular booklets (over one million were distributed in 1932) and texts, as well as organising national pilgrimages, public lectures, study clubs, etc. The Central Catholic Library, apart from having an impressive collection of religious books, also organised various activities. Catholic imagery and icons were typically present in most households – statues of Our Lady of Lourdes, images of the Sacred Heart, pious medals, rosary beads, etc. These religious objects along with the various Catholic organisations, provided a very strong cultural identity and Catholicism had long been a very significant component in the construction of an Irish identity.

There was also a tradition of devotional cults to local figures of piety such as Matt Talbot and St Charles of Mount Argus (only recently canonised). Organisations such as the St Vincent de Paul Society (whose founder, Sir Joseph Glynn, was a chairman of one of the Congress sub-committees) and the Legion of Mary (founded in 1921) were increasing in strength and the Legion, in particular, benefited greatly from the Congress as it provided an excellent opportunity to establish international contacts. Many very distinguished prelates attended a reception at the Legion's Regina Coeli Hostel and complimented the work done by the Legion, while expressing their hope that branches would be established in their native dioceses. With the expansion of various Catholic organisations in this period, the ultimate effect was an increase in levels of devotion, however short-lived. Diarmuid Ferriter has argued that in the long run the mass demonstrations of faith in this period (the Congress being the most spectacular example) may have ultimately worked to the detriment of the Church, as these great displays led to the Church being 'held in awe to an excessive degree'

Éamon de Valera with the Papal Legate during the Congress. (*Courtesy of Dublin Diocesan Archives, Eucharistic Congress Collection.*)

and contributed to 'the discouragement of diversity and questioning in matters of faith'. In terms specifically of the congress, the latter claim seems unfair given firstly that the Congress witnessed many of the greatest intellectuals and thinkers in the Church gathering to discuss core issues of faith in front of very large audiences in Dublin. Surely the Congress was also a celebration of the very diversity and global nature of the Church? One might recall here the wonderful image of a packed and beautifully decorated St Francis Xavier church with three almost otherworldly Churchmen, amid burning incense, celebrating Mass in the Byzantine/Slavonic Rite to a captivated, mainly Dublin congregation.

Although it is sometimes noted that the Congress must have further fostered a sense of exclusion among non-Catholics in the Free State (namely Protestants) – the many Protestant business people (including the Guinness family) who contributed generously to the Congress are forgotten. So too are the young Protestants who gathered to witness events such as the

Papal Legate's entry into Dublin – likely just as enthralled by the spectacle as Catholic youths. Regardless of religion, many would have found the greatly enlivened atmosphere and colour of the city very attractive. The Church of Ireland Archbishop of Dublin was one of those who warmly welcomed the Congress. The young children (mainly Protestant) who attended the Central Model School in Marlborough Street opposite the Pro-Cathedral also appear to have greatly enjoyed the excitement created the by Congress, as a student in the school at that time recently revealed to the author. Ten years after the establishment of an independent Irish state, despite a Catholic majority of approximately 93 per cent of the population in 1932, Protestants remained strikingly over-represented in the higher professions in the state, or indeed as employers, managers and foremen in industry, farmers holding over 200 acres, bank officials, etc. Although faith and fatherland interpretations of Irish history were common (the Catholic 'triumph over oppression') the Congress presented no real threat to the status quo but it certainly provided a strong impression that the vast majority of Catholics were very attached to their religious culture. This was in marked contrast to the serious decline in religious practice among most of the Protestant Churches in this period.

Éamon de Valera with Dr John Charles McQuaid, President of Blackrock College. (*Courtesy of Dublin Diocesan Archives, Eucharistic Congress Collection.*)

De Valera and the Congress

On a political level, the Congress proved fortuitous for the recently elected Fianna Fáil minority government, in particular for the new president, Éamon de Valera. Excommunicated from the Church due to his active support for the republican side during the Civil War in 1922 (a figurehead to some but not a military leader), the Congress provided de Valera with the opportunity to demonstrate his Catholic *bona fides* – very important given the overwhelmingly Catholic population of the state. Concerns about de Valera extended even to the Vatican at this time (due, in particular, to an Irish envoy who repeatedly presented a negative impression of him until his recent election victory). However, de Valera remained a devout Catholic throughout his life and even during the Civil War he continued to enjoy the friendship of a number of Churchmen.

In 1932 he was on very friendly terms with the young President of Blackrock College, Dr John Charles McQuaid (future Archbishop of Dublin), who hosted the great garden party to welcome the Papal Legate to Dublin. Photographs of de Valera at this event reveal him to have been in convivial form, comfortable exchanging greetings and pleasantries with the various prelates – many of whom he would have already met while on political tours of America, Britain and elsewhere. He made an impressive bilingual speech (speaking in Irish and Latin) during the state reception for the Papal Legate in Dublin Castle on the following evening, and was very frequently photographed participating in the Congress. De Valera maintained a very high profile throughout and by the close of events there was no doubting his Catholic loyalties. This ultimately helped to consolidate de Valera's remarkable political appeal, with his distinct blend of traditional Gaelic Catholic nationalism attracting many voters. Calling a snap election six months after the Congress de Valera's party was extremely successful and, as a result, was able to form a majority Government which would serve a full term and remain in office (in both majority and minority Governments) until 1948.

De Valera also used the occasion of the Congress to deliver a serious snub to the representative of the British Crown in the Irish Free State (theoretically the chief executive officer of the state), the Governor-General, James MacNeill. De Valera had already declared his intention to terminate such links with the Crown, which were written into the Free State Constitution in 1922. Shortly after assuming office in 1932 two of de Valera's ministers (Frank Aiken and Seán T. O'Kelly), in a blatant affront, walked out of a function held by the French Legation in Dublin when MacNeill and his wife arrived. Although MacNeill had been very prominent in the Catholic Emancipation centenary celebrations in 1929 (hosted by a different Government), in the run up to the Congress in 1932 de Valera expressed dismay at MacNeill's stated intention of having several 'distinguished European Catholics' as guests during the Congress, with de Valera noting the embarrassment to the Government. It was further stressed that the Government would be unable to assist the Governor-General in inviting any other visitors. During the garden party at Blackrock College, special measures were taken by Dr McQuaid (at the request of de Valera) to minimise, wherever possible, contact between himself and MacNeill.

Astonishingly, the Governor-General was not invited to the lavish state reception to welcome the Papal Legate in Dublin Castle. Given such treatment it was hardly surprising that the situation came to a head later in the year and, following a rather sensational protest over his

The Governor-General James MacNeill in formal dress to the left, making his way to the Pro-Cathedral during the Congress. John McCormack can be seen following behind on right. (*Courtesy of Dublin Diocesan Archives, Eucharistic Congress Collection.*)

treatment, MacNeill was forced to resign. He was soon afterwards replaced by a personal choice of de Valera himself, Domhnall ua Buachalla, who would fully comply with de Valera's wish to dramatically lower the profile of the Governor-General, until the position was terminated altogether following the Constitution Amendment Act in 1936.

As regards old Civil War animosities, the Congress undoubtedly aided the process of healing. De Valera and W.T. Cosgrave stood across from one another as canopy bearers during the procession of the Blessed Sacrament. After the ceremonies the Guard of Honour attended a dinner with the new Fianna Fáil Government – two groups who had fought on opposite sides during the Civil War. There was understandably some tension at first, but Éamon de Valera's gesture of inviting the officer in charge to sit at his side during the meal seemed to quickly change the atmosphere. The sense of common purpose and identity became foremost on the occasion.

Northern Ireland

In terms of a broader significance, the Congress highlighted a fundamental difference between the Irish Free State and Northern Ireland, where some Catholics travelling to the

Congress were attacked by loyalist mobs. Congress flags in Catholic areas were often torn down, damaged or destroyed. In some cases deliberately provocative banners, intended to insult Catholics and the Congress, were displayed on streets. An unpleasant situation which arose in the village of Donemana, Co. Tyrone, illustrates how Northern Ireland in this period could be, to say the least, a 'cold house' for Catholics. An Orange service was planned to take place in Donemana on 26 June (the penultimate day of the Congress in Dublin), and was attended by over 300 people who had come from all over the surrounding district and who planned to march through the village after the service. Part of the route from the church through the village was lined by Congress flags. The Orange brethren made it known in advance to the local District Inspector that they refused to pass under such decorations while also refusing to take any other route from the church. The District Inspector requested that the flags and arches on the particular road be taken down. Some Catholics objected to this. As the service in the church proceeded, a large group of Catholics began to gather in the village. The District Inspector called in reinforcements. On leaving the church the Orange brethren were informed that a hostile crowd had gathered in the village but they expressed their determination to march along the street. As they made their way along the road a melee broke out with bottles being thrown and several shots fired. Although the police managed to restore peace, wild scenes were witnessed later in the day with many of the Congress decorations in the town being torn down with a large crowd of loyalists gathering afterwards to sing 'God save the King'.

Some of the worst scenes were witnessed as Congress pilgrims from the North returned home. Although the Bishop of Down and Connor, Revd Dr Mageean (who participated prominently in the Congress) and the Nationalist MP Joseph Devlin (selected as one of the distinguished canopy bearers during the procession of the Blessed Sacrament) sent messages to the Minister of Home Affairs, Sir Dawson Bates, demanding adequate protection for the returning pilgrims, that message was not sufficiently heeded. It was estimated that approximately 500 loyalists gathered outside the Central Train Station in Belfast, many with bottles and other missiles to attack the pilgrims. In Larne those returning on the ferry from Dublin were attacked. Groups of stone-throwers had already attacked the same passengers as they embarked for Dublin a few days previously when about a dozen pilgrims, most of whom were women, were injured either by stones or broken glass. At Ballymena buses were attacked and windows smashed. Similar scenes took place in Coleraine and many other towns and villages in the North. Two weeks later, main streets in most Northern towns were profusely decorated with loyalist symbols for the Twelfth of July celebrations. There was no record of any damage to these decorations.

The charge that the Eucharistic Congress, being such a vibrant Catholic celebration in Dublin, so thoroughly embraced at every level in the Free State, could only serve to further consolidate the partition of Ireland, is undeniable. However, it should be stressed, opposition to a united Ireland was a long-held bedrock political stance among Protestant unionists in Northern Ireland and, in a psychological and very real sense, partition was firmly entrenched at this stage. In that regard the Congress did not offer any threat, only further confirmation, if needed, of existing beliefs. It has even been suggested that the unionist political elite quietly admired the Congress. (Although no unionist MP from the North attended, all Northern Ireland MPs were invited to the Congress. Frank O'Reilly had actually grown up in the

Falls Road area of Belfast.) Media coverage from Belfast was overwhelmingly favourable and extensive. The pomp and the ceremony involved in welcoming the Papal Legate in the south was akin to a royal visit elsewhere. No visit of any British monarch to Belfast had yet been carried off with such *élan* and lessons could be learnt from the planning and organisation of the Congress. However, in truth, the only subsequent 'royal' visit to Ireland to compare in scale and popular enthusiasm with that of the was the visit of a Polish ecclesiastic in 1979, who had recently been elected Sovereign Pontiff (head of the Holy Roman Apostolic See) and titled, Pope John Paul II.

Mementoes and Souvenirs of the Congress

There are many artefacts and remnants of the Congress to be found around Dublin and elsewhere in Ireland. Immediately after the Congress, hundreds, if not thousands, of items (such as the furniture in the Hibernian Military School used by the prelates attending the ceremonies in the park) which had served their purpose during the Congress went onto the market and it was a feast for souvenir hunters. Whereas the great altar in the Phoenix Park was shortly afterwards dismantled and the building materials apparently recycled (though pieces from it survive all over the country), the O'Connell Bridge altar survives today, intact if not in situ, in the grounds of the Cappagh Orthopaedic Hospital in Finglas. Sr M. Polycarp, a Ward Sister at the Hospital, approached Archbishop Byrne immediately after the Congress about the possibility that the altar might be rebuilt, piece by piece, in Cappagh. Byrne was pleased with the idea and the altar was duly rebuilt and completed before Christmas the same year, with some modifications to ensure a more enduring structure.

The church of Christ the King at Cabra was referred to as a monument to the Eucharistic Feast of 1932 when the foundation stone was laid by Archbishop Byrne in September. Large crowds flocked to the ceremony and there were extensive decorations put up for the occasion.

Two beautiful examples of the Congress crest survive in the Pro-Cathedral, below the gallery and in the Parish Office. Congress crosses also still remain on the gates of St Joseph's church, Berkeley Road and at the Holy Family church, Aughrim Street (both churches are situated on one of the processional routes used in 1932). A street in Glasthule (close to Dún Laoghaire) was named Congress Gardens shortly after the Congress. In a number of cases throughout Ireland Congress crosses featured as decorative pieces on the walls of houses built in 1932, such as at Greenlands, Rosses Point, Co. Sligo. It has been suggested to the author that the street plan of houses on Clonmacnoise Road and Bangor Road in Crumlin (with a large circular green in the middle of the intersection of the two long roads) is based on the Congress cross. The religious theme of the street names in the surrounding area appears to support this.

A great chair used by the Papal Legate is featured in the Dublin Civic Museum collection. A beautiful chalice presented by the pontifical mission to the Archbishop of Dublin, along with surplices, processional torches and the monstrance used during the great procession in 1932, is still safely preserved in the Pro-Cathedral. Congress supplements and souvenir numbers which were produced by most Irish newspapers and journals have been preserved by many people, as have official Congress publications: the Advance Programme; the Hymn Book; the Congress Handbook; Programme of Events; official Congress badges; souvenir postcards (a wonderful series was produced in 1932 for visitors); souvenir plates; posters; tea towels; table cloths; napkins; handkerchiefs, and more have been treasured.

The Knock House Museum in Co. Mayo includes many interesting examples of Congress memorabilia. Many people compiled their own Congress scrapbooks in 1932 from newspaper cuttings, etc. A very popular *Pictorial Record* of the Congress was produced in 1933 by Veritas and copies can still be found in households throughout the country. Canon Boylan's account of the Congress, *The Book of the Congress*, was published the following year, though it was nothing like as successful as the *Pictorial Record*. Nonetheless, a second volume of the *Book of the Congress* containing the papers and addresses of the foreign sectional meetings was published in 1934. There exists ample newsreel footage of the Congress, which can be seen in both the Irish Film Centre Archives and the RTÉ Library. The Central Catholic Library contains some very interesting material relating to the Congress, as does the National Archives and the National Library. Finally, the Dublin Diocesan Archives contains twenty-five boxes full of Congress related material.

Various Congress souvenirs, including a piece from the altar in Phoenix Park. (*Courtesy of Knock Museum.*)

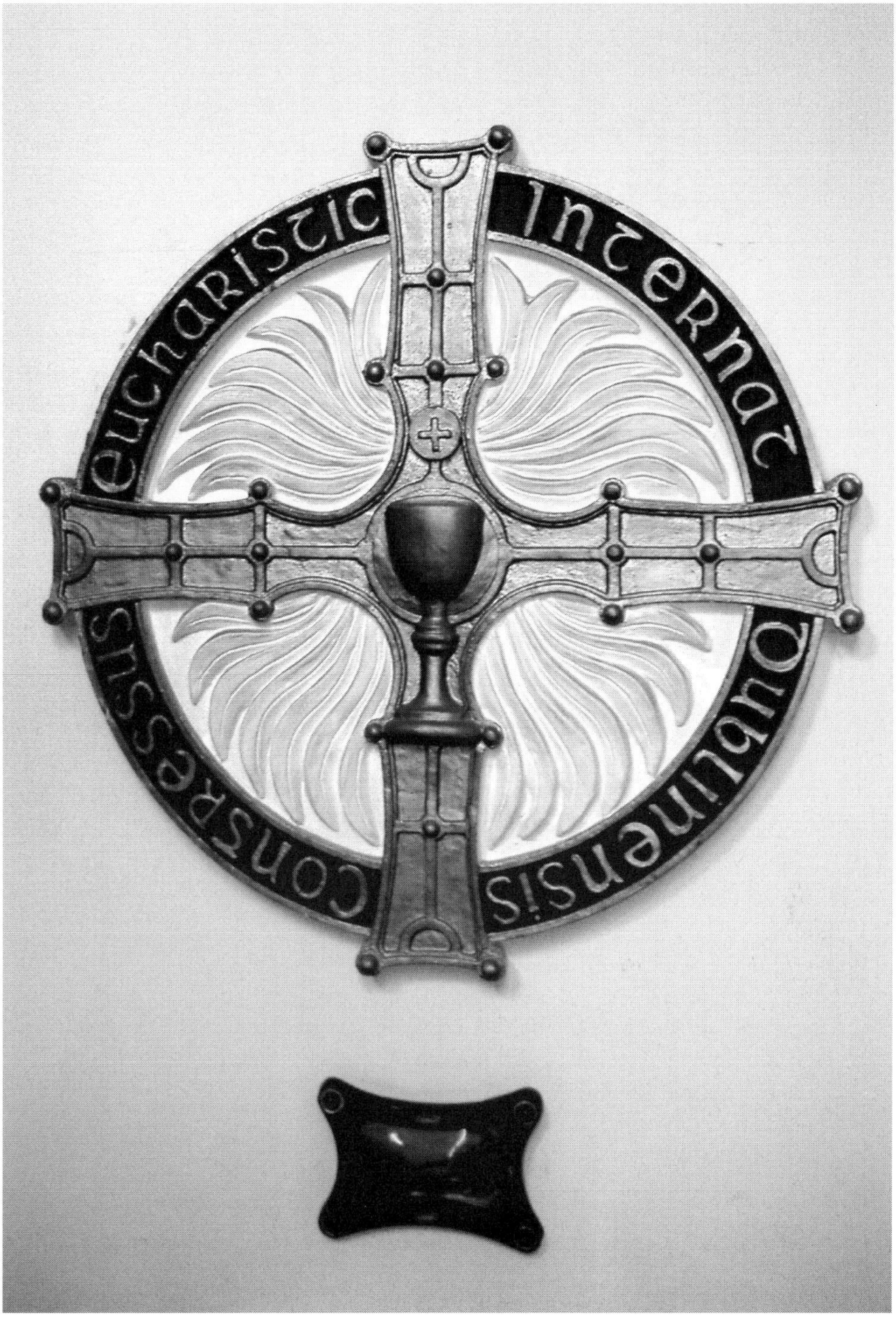

Congress Crest at Pro-Cathedral, Parish Office.(*Rory O'Dwyer.*)

The Book of the Congress, published in 1933. (*Courtesy of Dublin Diocesan Archives, Eucharistic Congress Collection.*)

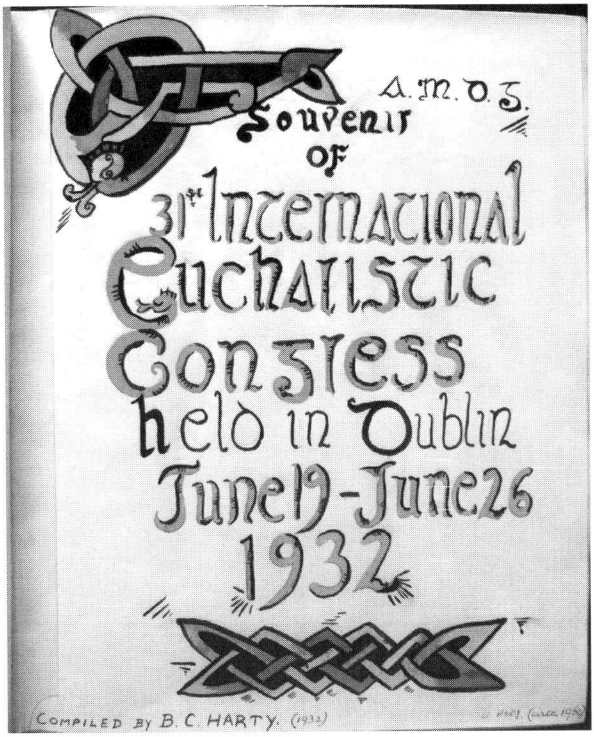

Eucharistic Congress scrapbook compiled by B.C. Harty in Cork. (*Courtesy of Ursula Fry.*)

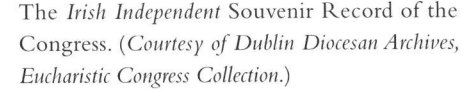

The *Irish Independent* Souvenir Record of the Congress. (*Courtesy of Dublin Diocesan Archives, Eucharistic Congress Collection.*)

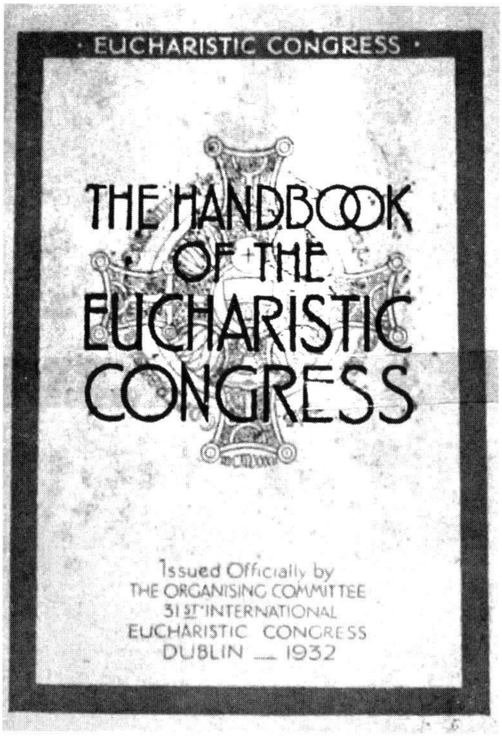

The Eucharistic Congress Handbook; a gem of information for the discerning Congress pilgrim. (*Courtesy of Knock Museum.*)

The Eucharistic Congress Hymn Book. Contains popular hymns (in English and Irish) such as ‘Faith of our Fathers’, ‘God Bless our Pope’ ‘Hail, Glorious St Patrick’, ‘Sweet Heart of Jesus’ and ‘Soul of my Saviour’, along with various Latin hymns. (*Courtesy of Knock Museum.*)

Above: Miniature Congress flag waved by a very young Mary Bennett on Main Street, Blackrock, as the Papal Legate passed her house on 20 June 1932. (*Courtesy of Mary Bennett.*)

Right: Chalice which was presented to the Archbishop of Dublin by the Pontifical Mission from Pope Pius XI. (*Rory O'Dwyer.*)

The O'Connell Bridge Congress altar at Cappagh Hospital, Finglas. (*Courtesy of Dublin Diocesan Archives.*)

Ornate urinal on Eden Quay, one of a number imported from France and erected along the city quays for the Congress. None of the urinals now survive *in situ* as they contravened hygiene regulations. The last was sold to an art student in the 1970s. (*Courtesy of Diarmuid Ó Gráda.*)

Epilogus

The Pope's visit in 1979, very interesting though it was in many respects, did not see a return to the same depth of religious feeling that had been witnessed in 1932. Levels of religious devotion and practice in Ireland had declined markedly since the 1930s. There would be no mighty Crusade of Prayer in preparation for the Pope's arrival. Although great crowds gathered in 1979, there was not the same sense of a nation (albeit the Catholic nation) proudly on show to the world. There was not the same virtual absence of cynicism. There could not be the same post-Civil War healing value. There was not the same fervent desire to send out a vibrant positive message to an international audience. There was not the same sense of a nation at prayer. The Congress in 1932 saw the most remarkable fusion of state, nation and religion. Even if it may not have necessarily been 'the greatest moment in the religious history of Ireland' as many journalists and some members of the clergy proclaimed during the event, it was certainly the greatest festival in Irish history.

Seventy-seven years on, Eucharistic Congresses continue to take place, generally every four years in recent times. The last Congress (the forty-ninth) took place in Quebec, Canada in June 2008 and was attended by approximately 12,000 people (a tiny number compared to the Dublin Congress). On the final day of that Congress, during the final Mass, Pope Benedict XVI (speaking via live video-link from Rome) announced during his homily that Dublin will host the Fiftieth Eucharistic Congress in 2012. It will mark the eightieth anniversary of the 1932 Congress as well as the fiftieth anniversary of the opening of the Second Vatican Council (which may relate to the theme for the 2012 Congress). Expectations of a papal visit for the Congress may prove unfounded. The Pope has usually been represented by a special Papal Legate at the Congresses. Although all appear to accept that the next Dublin Congress could not see a repeat of the spectacular displays of devotion witnessed in 1932, it is hoped that it will be an enriching and rewarding experience for all who choose to participate.

***

Chesterton on Dublin

There is nothing that I enjoy so much, in the ordinary way, as taking a ticket and a train and a boat and going to Dublin. There is much in Dublin of what has always been said about Paris. It is an indescribable liveliness and lucidity; as if it were morally what it is certainly not materially; the 'ville lumière'; the legendary place in the sun. But there is something else to understand, about the extraordinary experience of the thing called a Eucharistic Congress. It was not merely this; perhaps it was not mainly this. It was something altogether different and astonishing; though it doubtless included this. I did not merely take a ticket for Holyhead, or a boat for the port of Dublin.

I did truly take a ticket for Christendom. I took a train and a boat that brought me to the ancient, and perhaps long-undiscovered, island that was once called Christendom. For it did truly appear, as in a dream, that the island had grown large, and that I had landed on something larger than a continent. For Christendom is much larger than Europe. Even in the Middle Ages it was much larger than Europe. I am not arguing here about the claims of various sorts of Christians to inherit the full tradition of Christendom. I only say that to see even so much of Christendom in one place was like seeing a vision; like being taken to the top of a mountain and seeing all the kingdoms of the earth. If any bright wit from Portadown or Belfast retorts that the Devil, in the person of the Papal Legate, would naturally take me there, I am content to bow and smile.

(*Christendom in Dublin*, pp21–22.)

Appendix

Programme of the Congress

Sunday 5 June
Retreats for women begin in all churches of the City of Dublin and the Coastal Borough.

Sunday 12 June
General Communion for Women throughout Ireland. Close of retreats for Women in all the churches of the City of Dublin and the coastal Borough. Retreats for Men begin in all churches in the City of Dublin and in the coastal Borough.

Sunday 19 June
General Communion of Men throughout Ireland. Close of Retreats for men in all churches of the City of Dublin and the coastal borough.
8p.m. – Triduum for the success of the Congress begins in all the churches of the Archdiocese of Dublin.

Monday 20 June
Afternoon – arrival of the Cardinal Legate at Dún Laoghaire. Reception by the Archbishop of Dublin, the president and members of the Executive Council, representatives of the council of the borough and of the Congress committee. Triumphal procession to city boundary, where the Cardinal is received by the Lord Mayor of Dublin and the city Corporation, and conducted to the Pro-Cathedral, where he will be received by the Archbishop of Dublin, the bishops of Ireland and the Metropolitan Chapter of Dublin.
8p.m. – Triduum continues.

Tuesday 21 June
(On this day is solemnised the Feast of St Aloysius, patron of Youth.) General Communion for children throughout Ireland.
3p.m. – Garden party at Blackrock College given by the Archbishops and bishops of Ireland in honour of the Cardinal Legate.

8p.m. – Triduum closes.
9.30p.m. – State Reception in honour of the Cardinal Legate at St Patrick's Hall, Dublin Castle.

Wednesday 22 June
3p.m. – Formal opening of the Congress at the Pro-Cathedral by the Cardinal Legate.
9p.m. to Midnight – Exposition of the Blessed Sacrament in every church in the city of Dublin and suburbs concluding with Benediction of the Blessed Sacrament.
Illumination of the city from dusk till dawn.

Thursday 23 June
12.30a.m. – Midnight Mass in all churches of the City of Dublin and suburbs.
11a.m. – Solemn Pontifical High Mass, Pro-Cathedral.
12.30p.m. – Meeting for Priests (in Latin), Mansion House.
Exposition of the Blessed Sacrament held in many churches in the city of Dublin from the conclusion of last Mass until 2p.m.

General Meetings
3p.m. – In Irish, Theatre Royal. [Note: Irish as printed in 1932] Leigheacht: 'Na Seana Ghaedhil agus Corp Críost,' An t-Athair Risteárd Phléimeann. (Address: 'The Ancient Gael and the Blessed Sacrament' by Revd Richard Fleming.) Chairman: The Bishop of Down and Connor.

In English, Savoy Theatre. Addresses: 'The Holy Eucharist in Early Ireland' by Dr Eoin MacNeill, and 'The Holy Eucharist in Medieval Ireland', by Revd John Ryan, SJ. Chairman: The Archbishop of San Francisco.
8p.m. – Mass Meeting of Men in Phoenix Park – the Cardinal Legate presiding. Leigheacht: 'An t-aifreann Laetheamhail,' Easboc Ro-Urramach Ratha Bhoth ('Daily Mass', by the Bishop of Raphoe). Address in English: 'The Blessed Eucharist the Sacrament of Charity and Peace,' by the Archbishop of St Louis. Hymns in Irish and English. Benediction of the Most Blessed Sacrament given by the Cardinal Legate.

Friday 24 June
11a.m. – Solemn Pontifical Mass, Pro-Cathedral.
Exposition of the Blessed Sacrament held in many churches in the city of Dublin from the conclusion of last Mass until 2p.m.

General Meetings
3p.m. – In Irish, Theatre Royal. Leigheacht: 'Ruindiamhair Cuirp Chriost i n-Eirinn o thus an chreidimh ghallda go dti an la indiu', An t-Athair P. MacGiolla Cearr. (Address: 'Mysteries of the Blessed Eucharist in Ireland from the introduction of the Alien Faith to the Present Day', by Revd P. Kerr.) Chairman: The Bishop of Raphoe.

In English, Savoy Theatre. Addresses: 'The Holy Eucharist in Ireland during the Persecutions', by Professor J.M. O'Sullivan, TD, and 'The Holy Eucharist in Modern Ireland by Mgr McCaffrey. Chairman: The Bishop of Southwark.

8p.m. – Mass Meeting of women in the Phoenix Park – the Cardinal Legate presiding. Leigheacht: 'Cuarta ar an t-Sacraimint Ró-Naomhtha', Easboc Ro-Urramach Dhúin agus Choinnire ('Visits to the Blessed Sacrament,' by the Bishop of Down and Connor.) Address in English: 'Frequent Communion', by the Archbishop of Manila, Revd Dr O'Doherty. Hymns in Irish and English. Benediction of the Blessed Sacrament given by the Cardinal Legate.

Saturday 25 June

12 noon – Solemn Pontifical High Mass for Children. Phoenix Park. Cardinal Legate presiding.

Sunday 26 June

1p.m. – Solemn Pontifical Mass, Phoenix Park.
Procession of the Blessed Sacrament: the Blessed Sacrament borne in solemn procession by the Papal Legate from the altar in the Phoenix Park to the altar on O'Connell Bridge.
Benediction given at O'Connell Bridge.
(This above list does not include the very large number of sectional meetings for foreign groups.)

Pupils at the Presentation Convent School, George's Hill, enjoying the special Congress atmosphere. Most of them would never forget the event. It was a touchstone in their lives. (*Courtesy of National Library of Ireland.*)

Personal Recollections

This is a selection of correspondence received by the author in response to a letter published in most Irish newspapers in May 2008, seeking contact with people who participated in the Congress.

Tralee
19/5/08

I was present at the Eucharistic Congress in Dublin in 1932. I was a member of the first Kerry Troup of the Catholic Boy Scouts. I can remember the weather was very warm and as a result I got a bad sunburn on my arms. We had to do duty at the ceremonies in the Phoenix Park and at O'Connell Bridge. During our hours of duty we had to roll up the sleeves of our tunics – hence the sunburn. Thousands of Boy Scouts from all parts of Ireland were camped in the grounds of Terenure College. The food was not great but we had plenty of football and hurling. I was very lucky to be picked on the National Guard of Honour which was formed up near the High Altar during the Masses in the Park and on O'Connell Bridge. I had the honour to be very close to Count John McCormack when he sang 'Panis Angelicus'. I also had the honour of seeing Éamon de Valera greet William Cosgrave as they were taking their places. It was less than ten years since the end of our Civil War. So the Congress was a wonderful help to unite people and leaders of all the different parties at the time.

There was a big garden party held in the Blackrock College grounds in honour of the Papal Legate. I was on duty there with some of my comrades. We worked hard in the very warm weather but we were rewarded with a good supply of ice cream and nice cookies.

I am now in my ninety-third year but I can remember the Congress and the many incidents – as if it was only a year ago. It was a wonderful occasion for our Church and our country and as a turning point in our history. I hope that I am some help to you in your research. Kindly excuse my writing and spelling. Not as firm now as in the past.

Le gach-dea ghuí,
M.S.

Wexford
7/6/08

My late father's first cousin Fr John Toohey attended the Eucharistic Congress in 1932. He visited his father's birthplace – Scariff, Co. Clare. [Toohey had been ordained in Sydney, Australia in 1927. He was consecrated co-adjutor Bishop of Maitland in 1948 and succeeded to the see of Maitland in 1956.]

Another cousin (also from Clare) came to the Eucharistic Congress from Iowa, USA – Fr James Curtin. I have no information on him.

Yours sincerely,
G.M.

The above letter illustrates a very common experience during the Congress, of a relation in the religious life coming to stay.

Louis Hogan (right) with his younger brother in 1932. Louis was a member of the Palestrina Choir and sang at the High Mass in the Phoenix Park. Like so many of his peers he was greatly inspired by John McCormack and would cherish the privilege of having sung with McCormack at the Congress. (*Courtesy of Louis Hogan.*)

Medal given to members of the choir for the Pontifical High Mass in the Phoenix Park. (*Courtesy of Knock House Museum.*)

Roderick Reid (far right), pictured with his family in 1932, was a chief boy soprano in the choir at the Pontifical High Mass in the Phoenix Park. (*Courtesy of Marion Reynolds.*)

Catholic Boy Scouts having lunch at their camp in the grounds of Terenure College. Approximately 2,000 Scouts camped at the site. A smaller camp site existed for Girl Guides from around Ireland at the Powerscourt Estate, Co. Wicklow. (*Courtesy of Dublin Diocesan Archives, Eucharistic Congress Collection.*)

Dublin
18/5/08

I was thirteen years of age and a pupil in St Michael's CBS in Inchicore. In 1932, there was a great air of excitement all over the country and especially in Dublin in the weeks leading up to the climax of the Congress. Crowds of people arrived in Dublin by sea and train. Dignitaries from all over the world poured into Dublin. The Pope appointed an Italian Cardinal Lauri as his representative for the Congress. He received a wonderful welcome on his arrival in Dún Laoghaire. The entire route from Dún Laoghaire into the city was lined by schoolchildren, all waving Papal flags. The pupils at my school were located along Morehampton Road. We were dressed in a uniform for the first time (a blue blazer, grey short trousers, school tie and a distinctive skull cap). The Papal Legate was accompanied into Dublin by a mounted guard of honour. They were members of the Army cavalry and they were resplendent in their blue ceremonial uniforms and hussar headdress.

In the week before the Congress Mass religious services took place all over Dublin and I remember the special midnight Mass in the Oblate church in Inchicore. I lived in an area of

Troop of Scouts from Athlone who offered their services for the Congress and would have camped at Terenure College. (*Courtesy of Gearóid O'Brien.*)

George Fitzgerald, pictured here with his wife and children outside their house on Madden Road in the Liberties during the Congress, was one of the 20,000 stewards who helped ensure the Congress was a great success. (*Courtesy of Frank Fitzgerald.*)

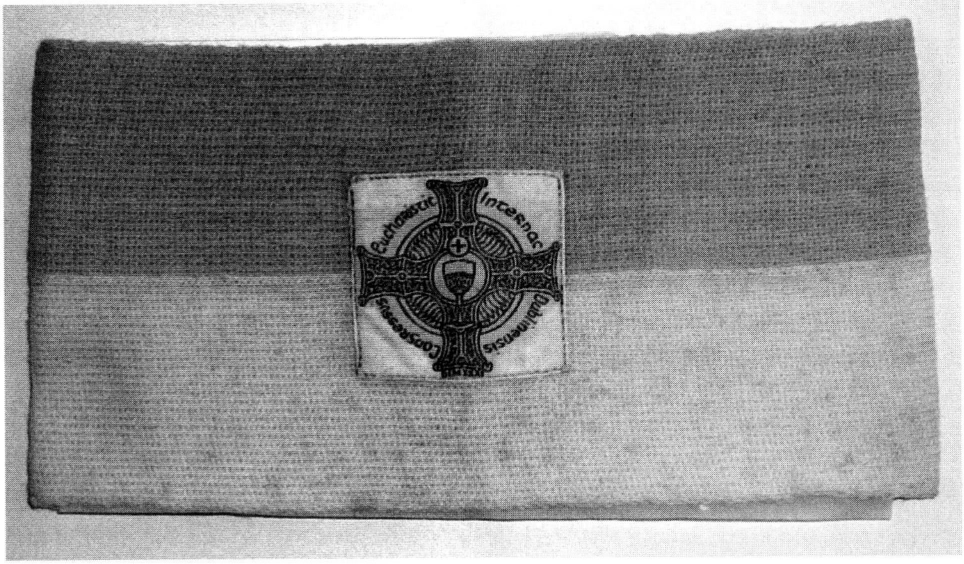

Stewards armlet for Congress. All stewards were requested to have armlets affixed to the left sleeve of their coats, midway above their elbows. The armlets were issued in the following colours: General Body – Yellow and White (with Congress crest in green); Liaison Officers – Blue and White with Congress Crest; Senior Officers (Assistant Marshals) – Orange with Congress Crest and title in blue, and Committee – Orange with Congress Crest and title in red. (*Courtesy of Knock Museum.*)

Members of St John's Ambulance providing assistance to a woman during a ceremony in the Phoenix Park. The brigade provided an excellent back-up service during the Congress. With the crowding, the heat and the sunshine at the open-air ceremonies, there were many instances of people fainting. Over 600 members offered their services during the Congress. (*Courtesy of the National Library of Ireland.*)

Inchicore known as 'the Ranch' and I will never forget the excitement and enthusiasm of the people. Every street and every avenue was decorated with bunting from one side of the street to the other side. Almost every house displayed three flags:

The papal flag of yellow and white with the keys of the kingdom on it.
The Congress flag of blue with a chalice on it.
The national flag of green, white and orange.

The men of the Ranch came out after their day's work and put up the decorations and Dick Horan, a carpenter from Inchicore Railway works, made window boxes for the people to display flowers. Of course the whole of Dublin and Inchicore was decorated. The Bishop of Lourdes came and stayed in the Oblate House of Retreat and Fr Sweeney, the Superior of Oblates in Ireland and himself a Canon of Lourdes was so proud of the efforts of the Inchicore people that he brought the bishop on a tour of all the districts of Inchicore. There was tremendous excitement when the Bishop of Lourdes arrived in the Ranch.

On the Saturday before the main ceremony, there was a gathering and Mass for children and the Papal Legate was driven down all the aisles so we could see him. Altars were erected in parts of Dublin; one on O'Connell Bridge and another at Parkgate Street. Benediction was given at those altars.

The climax of the Congress was the Mass in the Phoenix Park. The big iron gates leading into the Phoenix Park at Parkgate Street were removed and an archway constructed, which was covered in flowers. An enormous crowd of people attended the Mass and my greatest memory of that day is entering a field at the end of Park Street at the Ranch. A big hill descended from this field down to the Liffey and it was possible to see a section of the multitude of people in the Phoenix Park and to hear some of the ceremony which came across the Liffey from the amplification which carried the sound all over the park.

I heard John McCormack singing 'Panis Angelicus' and 'Ave Maria' during the Mass. The Papal Legate was driven in a car all over Dublin so that he could meet as many people as possible. After he had left Ireland this car was offered as first prize in a monster raffle.

L.K. (aged eighty-nine years).

Athy
20/5/08

On reading your letter requesting memories of the Eucharistic Congress – having just been confirmed by Archbishop Byrne and celebrating my tenth birthday that year – I took the notion of writing my recollections of that great event.

I remember seeing Dev and the new Irish Government joining the clergy in greeting the Cardinal Legate at the mail boat. That was a big occasion for me and thousands of others. Our town [Athy] was completely decorated with flags and bunting. I was considered too small to go to Dublin on the big Sunday. The people of Athy who could not go gathered in Athy People's Park and we heard it all on loudspeakers provided by Cpt. Hosie, who was Proprietor of I.V.I. Ltd, completely at his own expense. He procured the best broadcasting system that Siemens of Germany could provide. Cpt. Hosie was a great Athy man (and a Protestant) – a man who was before his time. The people of Athy were most grateful to him as money was scarce at that time. There were never so many 'prams' in the park at the same time before or since! It was great to hear the choir led by John McCormack (who we had often seen as he lived in Moore Abbey, Monasterevan at the time).

F. O'B.

Dublin
18/5/08

I was ten years old in 1932 and lived with my parents and siblings on Merrion Road about half a mile from the city and county boundary of Dublin. At this spot two tall towers were erected on either side of the road connected by an ornamental archway. The building of this was a source of awe and wonder to us children on our way to and from school. This was the route the Legate was to take from Dún Laoghaire, where he would arrive on the mail boat. As pupils at the local National School, my sister and I were among those chosen to line the route at this archway to the city, the local boys' school on one side of the road, the girls' on the other. I can't remember what the boys wore but the girls had a special outfit, yellow flared skirts with a white blouse (being the Papal colours) and a blue sleeveless bolero (blue being the Congress colour). We all had Congress badges and flags to wave.

We had to take our places very early on the day of the arrival of the Cardinal Legate, but there was a sense of great excitement as various dignitaries arrived to take their places on the platform and eventually we could hear the noise of the approaching cavalcade. And what a cavalcade it was, led by the army horse riders in their blue and gold uniforms, the cardinal in his red robes, the clanking of the bridles, the cheering of the crowds, the sheer excitement of it all. And then it had all passed on and, released by our teachers, my sister and I raced home because we knew there was excitement there too. Because our house offered a grandstand view of the processional route, our grandparents, uncles and aunts, and our cousins were all invited to our house. Our father, grandfather and uncles built a platform for the men folk. The ladies were all seated upstairs at the windows, with the children fitting in where they could. It was just one great day which I have never forgotten.

We got another chance to wear our papal outfits when we attended the Children's Mass in the Phoenix Park. We were bussed there from our school complete with packed lunch. When we arrived, and on the instruction of our teachers, we all sat down on the grass. There were thousands of children all around, nobody in papal colours, and it was many years later I realised that we had been privileged children. We had been in the right place at the right time to greet the Cardinal. However at the park we were just one of many. We were so far away from the altar.

A few days later our parents brought us into Dublin to see the flags and bunting and the high altar on O'Connell Bridge. We listened on the radio to John McCormack singing 'Panis Angelicus' at the High Mass in the park. And then the Eucharistic Congress was over. It was a unique event and a great time if you lived in Dublin.

N.T.

Belfast
26/6/08

My school was St Mary's PES, off the Falls Road. We travelled by train on a Saturday which was very special for children. We were dressed in our best with ribboned identification round our necks in the event of our wandering off or getting lost. We also wore a Eucharistic Cross which each of us were given. Being with school friends and having a meal on the train was a great novelty which we enjoyed immensely. Phoenix Park was so beautifully decorated for this big occasion and the choirs were heavenly. When John McCormack sang, well there are no words to describe it all.

The next day was Sunday, the closing day of the event. We lived in a street with many houses close together and two neighbours brought their wireless sets out to the windowsills so we could all hear the wonderful singing and the Pope blessing us all.

M.K.

Ardee
13/5/08

I was at the Eucharistic Congress in 1932. We went on a day trip on a special train from Ardee Station, my father and mother and the two eldest children – my older sister and myself. I was then eight and a half years old.

The Papal Legate was Cardinal Lauri. My mother was expecting a baby at the time – the baby was born on 20 August and she was named Lauri.

N.S.

Thousands of people travelled to Dublin by train on a day trip for the final day of the Congress. The rail network was more extensive then than it is today and numerous extra train services had to be provided. Trains departed from places such as Clonakilty, Co. Cork, from 3.40a.m. and continued through the early morning hours. From 5.00a.m. trains were departing every fifteen minutes from the Glanmire Station in Cork, with the trains entirely booked by different Cork parishes. Similar services were provided from other Irish cities and large towns. The atmosphere on the trains was very cheerful and hymns were frequently sung. Basic refreshments were usually available on these trains, such as a hot cup of Bovril (served in papier-mâché cups). Passengers typically brought their own lunch and picnicked later in the Phoenix Park immediately after Mass and before the procession began.

As regards the naming of the baby, many children, boys and girls, born in the months after the Congress were christened with the name Lauri (after the Papal Legate), either as a first or second name. Some girls were named Eucharia after the Eucharistic Congress.

Derry
20/5/08

My father attended the Eucharistic Congress and often spoke of hearing John McCormack singing 'Panis Angelicus'. I still have my father's lapel badge from the Congress after all the years. We had an old neighbour many years ago in Derry, a local barman called Willie Murray. My father told the story of Willie Murray and his wife who cycled to the Congress in 1932 on a tandem – some journey in those days. Willie was actually a founder member of the City of Derry Cycling Club in the 1920s.

B.R.

Many people from all over Ireland cycled to Dublin for the Congress. Most travelled with a group of cyclists. Some people also walked to Dublin even from very remote parts of Ireland – perhaps as a sort of penitential exercise. Indeed, with the accommodation crisis in Dublin, it was suggested that Kilmainham Gaol (vacant since 1924 and in a poor condition in 1932) could serve as a penitential hostel for Congress pilgrims. Close to the Phoenix Park and within easy reach of the city centre, the location at least was ideal. The gaol, however, remained closed.

Carrick, Co. Donegal
17/05/08

A number of people travelled from this parish to the Congress. The late James Maloney of Aughera told me how he travelled on J.W. Cunningham's lorry from Carrick to Dublin. He recalled how they borrowed some chapel seats from Canon Ward and fixed them on to the lorry. J.W. Cunningham himself drove the lorry to Bundoran and then Johnny Doherty of Carrick took over the driving. He drove to Dublin and back again to Carrick. On their way to Dublin on Saturday evening they stopped in Longford in a restaurant/pub for a meal. This business was owned by a man called Andrew Hegarty from Kilcar, father of Dermot Hegarty, the famous singer.

They attended the Papal Mass in the Phoenix Park and then travelled in to O'Connell Bridge for the liturgical ceremonies. Late on Sunday evening they began the long journey back to Carrick. James Maloney related that the weather was glorious – sunshine all the way. They were all delighted and overjoyed to see all the towns that they had never visited but heard about at school.

E.G.

Many people appear to have travelled to the Congress on the back of a truck or lorry and many old vehicles were probably brought out on the roads again when they may not have been in a roadworthy condition. Two sections of the of the Eucharistic Congress Act (see sections 4 and 6 in the following section) made an order authorising the use on public roads during the Congress period of mechanically propelled vehicles for which road tax licences were not in force. The greatest tragedy in association with the Congress was the crash of a lorry carrying a group of twenty-seven pilgrims returning to Tullamore from the Congress. At 3a.m. on Monday 27 June, the lorry crashed into a railing at the Salmon Leap Bridge in Leixlip, precipitating its occupants into the shallow river twenty feet below. Two passengers were killed and all of the others were injured, some very seriously. In another incident, an Italian priest, Fr Thomatis (visiting for the Congress) was struck by a car at High Street in the city centre. He died later that day from his injuries.

Dublin
9/6/08

I was ten years old in 1932 and because I was confirmed that year our class were given a special stand for the procession of the Papal Legate from Dún Laoghaire to the Pro-Cathedral. We were positioned at Merrion Square. We had a fantastic view of the outriders – the Cardinal in an open-topped car followed by no end of clergy, ministers and other dignitaries. The Cardinal, as far as I can recall, was in his full regalia. I would guess the procession took about fifteen minutes and we were so excited waving our papal flags.

Another memory I have is the ships from other countries docking on the south wall of the Liffey (we lived quite close); my friend's brother was a scout leader and his troop met some of these visitors and escorted them. Larry at the head, carrying the flag, followed by his troop, followed by the visitors. I haven't a clue where they went but it was somewhere in the city.

Group of cyclists from the Falls Road area about to set off on cycle to Dublin for the Congress. (*Courtesy of Dublin Diocesan Archives, Eucharistic Congress Collection.*)

All the houses in the parish flew two flags – the Papal flag and the Congress flag, which had a host printed on it. These flags were a must and I remember my mother going to the church weekly to pay something off the flags. No one could afford to pay outright. We lived on a main street and it was spectacular to see the flags flying. We kept these flags folded carefully for about forty years. All the houses, and believe me some of them were hovels, had the most colourful altars outside their doors. The people put all they had into them and you could scarcely walk on the footpaths. Of course, people were very religious and they understood what the Eucharistic Congress meant.

The final day was very special. Children were not allowed join but my mother was gone for the day with the women's sodality and all their banners. She came back exhausted but overjoyed. My father probably went with the men's sodality and recovered with a few pints in the local.

K.D.

Parents were discouraged from bringing children to the main Mass in the park but many of those who travelled from outside Dublin by train for the day or for a few days, brought their children with them.

Tramore
21/5/08

I was in the Park when I was nine years of age with my family up from Waterford. It was a very hot day and the lady we were staying with used the pony and trap to take people who fainted to the Red Cross Depot. It was a wonderful day. I remember the hymn-singing and the blessing by the Papal Legate after Mass. In school we made books all about the Congress. I still have mine.

M.H.

Belfast
25/5/08

I was a member of the boys' confraternity in Leonard Monastery run by the Redemptorist Order and our journey was organised by them. I was born in March 1921 and so was eleven years of age at that time. Several trains were engaged to take members of the women's, men's and boys' confraternities for the occasion. During the journey, decades of the Rosary were said in the carriages and during the journey the chap who was giving out the decades plaintively asked 'What's the third Glorious mystery?'

When we reached our destination at the station, we were lined up and marched through the unfamiliar streets of Dublin. The streets were lined with crowds of people, and we heard their comments, such as 'they're a fine body of boys – they must be from Cork or Kerry'. I got the impression that they were disappointed when they heard that instead, we were from the 'Black North'.

We finally reached the park where the ceremonies were to be held, and for me personally, it was an overwhelming experience – I was only eleven years of age at the time – and the whole panorama was never to be forgotten. There were hundreds of priests, nuns in various garbs, not to mention the bishops in their colourful clothes, huge tents for the thousands of cups of tea.

Altogether, it was a memorable and joyous occasion, and unfortunately I remember very little of the spiritual side of the occasion. I suppose that since it happened many moons ago, that is to be expected.

The journey home was uneventful for us – though I heard some returning trains were stoned going through Portadown – but I probably slept, after such a long and memorable day.

K.B.

Dublin
19/05/08

In 1932 I was fourteen years of age attending the Mercy Convent, Baggot Street. Our teacher, Sr Pius, organised our class along with many other schools in Dublin to sing at the Children's Mass on the Saturday. We practised every day and once went to the park for a rehearsal, really to get our places on the platform.

The day Cardinal Lauri arrived our school lined up on the north side of Merrion Square to greet him as he passed by from Dún Laoghaire. Every house had a papal flag flying and bunting across the streets. Townsend Street was outstanding. The walls surrounding the doors were painted blue and white, statues and holy pictures and flowers were in every window. There were altars on the pathways, plus all the flags and bunting. I remember the altar on O'Connell Bridge and the crowds of people gathered there on Sunday. The altar is now erected in the grounds of Cappagh Hospital.

W.Q.

Eucharistic Congress (Miscellaneous Provisions) Act, 1932

Number 7 of 1932
Eucharistic Congress (Miscellaneous Provisions) Act, 1932

An Act to make certain modifications in the Law for the purposes of the Eucharistic Congress to be held in the month of June, 1932. [15th June, 1932]

Be it enacted by the Oireachtas of Saorstát Éireann as follows:

Definitions

1. In this Act:

The expression 'the Congress period' means the period commencing on the 18th day of June, 1932, and ending on the 1st day of July, 1932;
The expression 'the Minister' means the Minister for Local Government and Public Health;
The expression 'driving licence' means a licence under section 3 of the Motor Car Act, 1903;
The expression 'the Judge' means a Judge of the Circuit Court for the time being assigned to the Circuit which includes the County Borough of Dublin;
The expression 'the Act of 1927' means the Intoxicating Liquor Act 1927 (No.15 of 1927); and,
The expressions 'licensing area', 'on-licence', 'hotel', and 'restaurant' have the same meanings as they have in Part II of the Act of 1927.

Exemption from motor car duty of omnibus imported for use during the Congress period

2. (1) Notwithstanding anything contained in section 56 of the Customs Consolidation Act, 1876, and in section 11 of the Finance Act, 1928 (no.11of 1928), the Revenue Commissioners may admit without payment of the duty imposed by section 11 of the Finance Act, 1928, as amended by or under any subsequent enactment any motor omnibus imported by a person resident in Saorstát Éireann during the Congress period which is intended to be exported after the expiration of the said period.
(2) The Revenue Commissioners may for the purposes of this section prescribe the conditions as to security, due exportation and otherwise to be observed by the importer, and if such importer fails to comply with those conditions he shall be guilty of an offence under the Customs Acts and shall be liable on summary conviction thereof to a fine equal to treble the value of the motor omnibus including the motor car duty imposed thereon by section 11 of the Finance Act, 1982, as amended by or under any subsequent enactment, or at the election of the Revenue Commissioners to a fine of one hundred pounds and in any case the motor omnibus in respect of which the offence is committed shall be forfeited to the State.
(3) In this section the expression 'motor omnibus' means a mechanically propelled vehicle which has seating accommodation for more than six persons exclusive of the driver.

Traffic regulations in Dublin City and County

3. (1) The Commissioner of the Garda Síochána may make regulations for the general

regulation and control of traffic on roads and for the prevention of obstruction or disorder thereon.

(2) Regulations made under this section may be limited in their application so as to apply:

(a) to specified classes of traffic only;

(b) on specified roads or portions of roads only; and,

(c) during specified periods or hours only.

(3) The power to make regulations under this section shall (without prejudice to the generality of such power) include power:

(a) to exclude traffic from roads;

(b) to appoint portions of roads to be used as parking places and to regulate the number of vehicles making use of such parking places and the conditions under which they may be used and to prohibit parking of vehicles in any portion of a road not so appointed;

(c) to prohibit the display on or in the neighbourhood of a road of any unauthorised notice giving any instruction or direction to traffic, and to provide for the immediate removal of any such notice; and,

(d) to prescribe the places at which and the maximum period for which omnibuses shall stop for the reception or setting down of passengers.

(4) Every person who does any act (whether of commission or omission) which is a contravention of a regulation made under this section shall be guilty of an offence under this section and shall on summary conviction thereof be liable to a fine not exceeding two pounds.

(5) Regulations made under this section shall have effect only in the County and City of Dublin and shall remain in force during the Congress period only.

(6) In this section the expression 'traffic' includes vehicles, and animals of every description, and pedestrians.

(7) Every regulation made under this section shall be published by the Commissioner of the Garda Síochána in such manner as he deems best for giving notice to the public.

Use of unlicenced motor cars

4. (1) The Minister may by order authorise, subject to such conditions (if any) as the Minister may specify in such order, the use on public roads during the Congress period of mechanically propelled vehicles either generally or of any specified class or classes or any specified mechanically propelled vehicle notwithstanding that a licence under section 13 of the Finance Act, 1920, as amended by subsequent enactments is not in force in relation to such vehicle.

(2) Where an order is made under this section it shall be lawful for any person subject to compliance with the conditions (if any) specified in such order to use during the Congress period, in case such order relates to mechanically propelled vehicles generally, any mechanically propelled vehicle, or, in case such order relates to a specified mechanically propelled vehicle, that mechanically propelled vehicle, notwithstanding that a licence under section 13 of the Finance Act, 1920, as amended by subsequent enactments, is not in force in relation to such vehicle and that any regulations made under section 12 of the Roads Act, 1920, are not complied with in relation to such vehicle.

Exemption from licensing of public-service vehicles in the Dublin Metropolitan Area

5. (1) During the Congress period it shall be lawful for any person subject to compliance with

such regulations (if any) as may be made by the Commissioner of the Garda Síochána to keep, ply, use or let to hire any vehicle in the Dublin Metropolitan Area notwithstanding that such vehicle is not licenced under Dublin Amended Carriage Act, 1854, or that no Dublin Plate is fixed thereto or that no plates, labels or marks which are or may be required to be fixed, painted or marked on any such vehicle in pursuance of the provisions in that behalf in the Dublin Carriage Act, 1853, are fixed, painted or marked thereon.
(2) In this section the expression 'the Dublin Plate' has the same meaning as it has in the Dublin Carriage Act, 1853.
(3) Every regulation made by the Commissioner of the Garda Síochána under this section shall be published by him in such a manner as he deems best for giving notice to the public.
(4) Nothing in this section shall render it lawful to use during the Congress period in the Dublin Metropolitan Area a mechanically propelled vehicle unless a licence under section 13 of the Finance Act, 1920, as amended by subsequent enactments is in force in relation to such vehicle or such vehicle may, under the immediately preceding section, be so used notwithstanding that such a licence is not in force in respect thereof.

Driving of motor cars by unlicenced persons

6. (1) The Minister may by order authorise, subject to such conditions (if any) as the Minister may specify in such order, the driving by any person or any person belonging to a specified class, of any motor car or any motor car of a specified class notwithstanding that such person is not the holder of a driving licence.
(2) Where an order is made under this section it shall be lawful for any person (other than a person who was the holder of a driving licence and whose licence is for the time being suspended under section 4 of the Motor Car Act, 1903, or a person who is for the time being disqualified under the said section 4 for obtaining a driving licence) to whom such order relates, subject to compliance with the conditions (if any) specified in such order, to drive during the Congress period, in case such order relates to any motor car, or in case such order relates to a motor car of a specified class, any motor car of that class notwithstanding that such person is not the holder of a driving licence.

Exemption of unlicenced persons acting as drivers and conductors in Dublin Metropolitan Area

7. (1) During the Congress period it shall be lawful in the Dublin Metropolitan Area for any person to act as a driver or conductor of any vehicle notwithstanding that such person is not the holder of a driver's licence or conductor's licence as the case may be granted under the Dublin Carriage Act, 1853, or does not wear any badge of distinction which is required to be worn in pursuance of the said Act.
(2) Nothing in this section shall render it unlawful for any person to drive during the Congress period in the Dublin Metropolitan Area a mechanically propelled vehicle unless such person is the holder of a driving licence or is exempted under the immediately preceding section from the obligation to hold a driving licence.

Area Exemption orders

8. (1) The Judge may, upon the application of the officer in charge of the Garda Síochána for

any licencing area (including a licencing area outside the County Borough of Dublin), if he is satisfied that it is desirable in the public interest that such order should be made, grant in respect of such licencing area or any particular part thereof an order exempting, subject to compliance with such conditions as the Judge may think proper, all holders of on-licences attached to premises in such area or part during any specified hours on any specified day or days in the Congress period from the provisions of the Act of 1927, relating to prohibited hours in respect of such premises and, where any such order relates to several such days, different hours may be specified in respect of different days.

(2) Whenever an order under this section is granted the holder of an on-licence attached to premises in the area to which such order relates shall if and so long as he complies with the conditions (if any) attached to such order be exempt during the hours specified in such order from any penalty for contravention of the provisions of the Act of 1927, relating to prohibited hours in respect of such premises but not from any other penalty under the said Act or any other Act.

Special exemptions for hotels or restaurants in the neighbourhood of Dublin

9. (1) The Judge may, if he so thinks fit, on the application of any person who is the holder of an on-licence for premises which are an hotel or a restaurant and are situate within a radius of twenty miles from the General Post Office, Dublin, and after hearing the officer in charge of the Garda Síochána for the licencing area in which such premises are situate, grant to such person, an order exempting, subject to compliance with such conditions as the Judge may think proper, such person during any specified hours on any specified day or days in the Congress period from the provisions of the Act of 1927 relating to prohibited hours in respect of such premises, and, where any such order relates to several such days, different hours may be specified in respect of different days.

(2) Any person to whom an order under this section has been granted shall, if and so long as he complies with the conditions (if any) attached to such order, be exempt during the hours specified in such order from nay penalty for contravention or the provisions of the Act of 1927, relating to prohibited hours in respect of the premises to which the order relates but not from any other penalty under the said Act or any other Act.

(3) An order shall not be granted under this section unless the applicant therefore has, not less than forty-eight hours before making the application served upon the officer in charge of the Garda Síochána for the licencing area in which the premises are situate a notice of his intention to apply for the order setting out his name and address and the premises and the times for which the order is sought.

(4) No special exemption order under section 5 of the Act of 1927, shall be made in relation to any premises which are an hotel or a restaurant are and situate in the Dublin Metropolitan Area in respect of the Congress period or any part thereof.

Occasional Licences

10. The following provisions shall have effect in relation to every occasional licence granted under section 13 of the Revenue Act, 1862, as amended by subsequent enactments, which is granted to any person in respect of premises situate in the County Borough of Dublin and for a period beginning on or after the 18th day of June, 1932, and ending on or before the 1st day of July, 1932 that is to say:

(a) such licence may be granted to commence immediately on the expiration of another such licence previously granted to the same person in respect of the same premises notwithstanding that such previously granted licence has not expired;
(b) such licence may be granted to commence immediately on the expiration of another such licence previously granted to the same person in respect of the same premises notwithstanding that such previously granted licence has not expired;
(c) sub-sections (2) and (3) of section 6 of the Act of 1927 shall not apply in respect of such licence, but in lieu thereof it is hereby enacted that no such licence shall be granted without the previous consent of the Judge and such consent shall only be given by the said Judge after hearing the officer in charge of the Garda Síochána for the licencing area;
(d) such licence may be granted in respect of and may extend (subject to or without any special conditions) to any time on Sundays;
(e) the said Judge may on the application of the officer in charge of the Garda Síochána for the licencing area and after reasonable notice to the holder of such licence revoke such licence, if he is satisfied that breaches of the law relating to the sale of intoxicating liquor have occurred on or in relation to the premises to which such licence relates.

Prohibition of sale of intoxicating liquor during certain hours on the 26th July, 1932

11. (1) Notwithstanding anything contained in the Act of 1927, or in any occasional licence, or in any order made under this Act, it shall not be lawful for any person in the Dublin Metropolitan Area or in any part of the County Borough of Dublin which is outside the Dublin Metropolitan Area to sell or expose for sale any intoxicating liquor or to open or keep open any premises for the sale of intoxicating liquor or to permit any intoxicating liquor to be consumed on licenced premises on the 26th day of June, 1932, between the hours of two o'clock and six o'clock in the afternoon.
(2) Every person who shall sell or expose for sale any intoxicating liquor or open or keep open any premises for the sale of intoxicating liquor or permit any intoxicating liquor to be consumed on licenced premises in contravention of this section shall be guilty of an offence under this section and shall be liable on summary conviction thereof to a fine not exceeding twenty pounds.

Sale of intoxicating liquor on certain vessels

12. (1) Nothing in the Licencing (Ireland) Acts, 1833 to 1929, shall be deemed to prohibit or restrict during the Congress period the sale of intoxicating liquor on vessels moored in Dublin Bay (including the harbours of Dublin and Dún Laoghaire) for the purposes of the Eucharistic Congress, ordered and paid for by persons *bona fide* residing on such vessels.
(2) In this section the word 'vessel' does not include a passenger vessel as defined by section 52 of the Finance (1909–10) Act, 1910.

Exclusion of portion of Congress period for purposes of legal proceedings

13. (1) The time of the prescribed period shall not be reckoned in the computation of the times appointed or allowed by rules of court for the giving of any notice, the doing of any act or thing, or the taking of any step in or in relation to any action or matter or legal proceeding

of any kind.
(2) Where, by virtue of any enactment limiting the time within which any specified class of proceedings, whether civil or criminal, may be instituted, the time within which any particular proceedings may be instituted would, but for this section, expire during the prescribed period, such time shall be and is hereby extended up to and including the 30th day of June, 1932.
(3) In this section the expression 'the prescribed period' means the period commencing on the 20th day of June 1932, and ending on the 27th day of June, 1932.

Expenses
14. All expenses of carrying this Act into effect shall, to such extent as may be sanctioned by the Minister for Finance, be paid out of moneys to be provided by the Oireachtas.

Short title
15. This Act may be cited as the Eucharistic Congress (Miscellaneous Provisions) Act, 1932.

Eucharistic Congress Postcard. (*Courtesy of Tony Behan.*)

Attendees

The following is a list of the Cardinals, Archbishops, Bishops, Abbots, and Superiors General of Religious Orders that were present at the thirty-first International Eucharistic Congress:

Cardinals:

His Eminence, Cardinal Bourne, Archbishop of Westminster.
His Eminence, Cardinal Dougherty, Archbishop of Philadelphia.
His Eminence, Cardinal Hayes, Archbishop of New York.
His Eminence, Cardinal Hlond, Primate of Poland.
His Eminence, Cardinal Lavitrano, Archbishop of Palermo.
His Eminence, Cardinal MacRory, Archbishop of Armagh.
His Eminence, Cardinal O'Connell, Archbishop of Boston.
His Eminence, Cardinal van Roey, Archbishop of Malines.
His Eminence, Cardinal Verdier, Archbishop of Paris.

Archbishops:

His Excellency, Most Revd Paschal Robinson, O.F.M., Apostolic Nuncio.
His Excellency, Most Revd Dr Byrne, Archbishop of Dublin.
His Excellency, Most Revd Dr Beckman, Archbishop of Dubuque.
His Excellency, Most Revd Dr Bussolari, Archbishop of Modena.
His Excellency, Most Revd Dr Cattaneo, Archbishop of Palmyra.
His Excellency, Most Revd Dr Cesarano, Archbishop of Aversa.
His Excellency, Most Revd Dr Cuccarollo, Archbishop of Otranto.
His Excellency, Most Revd Dr Curley, Archbishop of Baltimore.
His Excellency, Most Revd Dr Dobrecic, Archbishop of Antivar.
His Excellency, Most Revd Dr Dowling, O.P., Archbishop of Port of Spain.
His Excellency, Most Revd Dr Downey, Archbishop of Liverpool.
His Excellency, Most Revd Dr Duke, Archbishop of Vancouver.
His Excellency, Most Revd Dr Forbes, Archbishop of Ottawa.
His Excellency, Most Revd Dr Gilmartin, Archbishop of Tuam.
His Excellency, Most Revd Dr Glennon, Archbishop of St Louis.
His Excellency, Most Revd Dr Hanna, Archbishop of San Francisco.
His Excellency, Most Revd Dr Harty, Archbishop of Cashel.
His Excellency, Most Revd Dr Howard, Archbishop of Portland.
His Excellency, Most Revd Dr Mar Ivanios, Archbishop of Trivandrum.
His Excellency, Most Revd Dr Jansen, Archbishop of Utrecht.
His Excellency, Most Revd Dr Kelly, Archbishop of Sydney.
His Excellency, Most Revd Dr Kenealy, Archbishop of Simla.
His Excellency, Most Revd Dr Mackintosh, Archbishop of Glasgow.
His Excellency, Most Revd Dr McDonald, Archbishop of Edinburgh.
His Excellency, Most Revd Dr McNeill, Archbishop of Toronto.
His Excellency, Most Revd Dr Mignen, Archbishop of Rennes.

His Excellency, Most Revd Dr Mostyn, Archbishop of Cardiff.
His Excellency, Most Revd Dr O'Brien, Archbishop of Kingston.
His Excellency, Most Revd Dr O'Donnell, Archbishop of Halifax.
His Excellency, Most Revd Dr Pisani, Archbishop of Constantia.
His Excellency, Most Revd Dr Redwood, Archbishop of Wellington.
His Excellency, Most Revd Dr Roditch, Archbishop of Belgrade.
His Excellency, Most Revd Dr Sinnott, Archbishop of Winnipeg.
His Excellency, Most Revd Dr Skvireckas, Archbishop of Kaunas.
His Excellency, Most Revd Dr Stritch, Archbishop of Milwaukee.
His Excellency, Most Revd Dr Tonna, Archbishop of Smyrna.
His Excellency, Most Revd Dr Williams, Archbishop of Birmingham.

Bishops:
His Excellency, Most Revd Dr Alter, Bishop of Toledo.
His Excellency, Most Revd Dr Amigo, Bishop of Southwark.
His Excellency, Most Revd Dr Arana, ODC, Bishop of Vijayapuram.
His Excellency, Most Revd Dr Audollent, Bishop of Blois.
His Excellency, Most Revd Dr Bagnoli, Bishop of Avezzano.
His Excellency, Most Revd Dr Barrett, Bishop of Plymouth.
His Excellency, Most Revd Dr Barry, Bishop of St Augustine.
His Excellency, Most Revd Dr Bartolomasi, Bishop of Petra.
His Excellency, Most Revd Dr Beeckmeyer, Bishop of Ceylon.
His Excellency, Most Revd Dr Berning, Bishop of Osnabrück.
His Excellency, Most Revd Dr Biermans, Bishop of Gargara.
His Excellency, Most Revd Dr Brennan, Bishop of Richmond.
His Excellency, Most Revd Dr Broderick, Bishop of Pednellis.
His Excellency, Most Revd Dr Brown, Bishop of Pella.
His Excellency, Most Revd Dr Browne, Bishop of Cloyne.
His Excellency, Most Revd Dr Bucys, Bishop of Olympus.
His Excellency, Most Revd Dr Budavonovic, Bishop of Cidamus.
His Excellency, Most Revd Dr Bunoz, OMI, Bishop of Tentyris.
His Excellency, Most Revd Dr Byrne, Bishop of Toowoomba.
His Excellency, Most Revd Dr Cantwell, Bishop of Los Angeles and San Diego.
His Excellency, Most Revd Dr Carevic, Bishop of Dubrovnik (Ragusa).
His Excellency, Most Revd Dr Cársky, Bishop of Tagora.
His Excellency, Most Revd Dr Chaptal, Bishop of Isinda.
His Excellency, Most Revd Dr Chulaparambil, Bishop of Kottayam.
His Excellency, Most Revd Dr Codd, Bishop of Ferns.
His Excellency, Most Revd Dr Cohalan, Bishop of Cork.
His Excellency, Most Revd Dr Collier, Bishop of Ossory.
His Excellency, Most Revd Dr Coppo, Bishop of Paleopolis.
His Excellency, Most Revd Dr Costes, Coadjutor-Bishop of Angers.
His Excellency, Most Revd Dr Cotter, Bishop of Portsmouth.
His Excellency, Most Revd Dr Cowgill, Bishop of Leeds.

His Excellency, Most Revd Dr Crowley, Bishop of Dacca.
His Excellency, Most Revd Dr Cullen, Bishop of Kildare and Leighlin.
His Excellency, Most Revd Dr Czarneckij, Bishop of Lebedus.
His Excellency, Most Revd Dr Dechamps, Bishop of Thennesus.
His Excellency, Most Revd Dr Delalle, Vicar Apostolic of Natal.
His Excellency, Most Revd Dr d'Herbigny, Bishop of Ilium.
His Excellency, Most Revd Dr Diepen, Bishop of 's-Hertogenbosch.
His Excellency, Most Revd Dr Dignan, Bishop of Clonfert.
His Excellency, Right Revd Dr Dobson, Bishop of Cinopolis.
His Excellency, Most Revd Dr Doorly, Bishop of Elphin.
His Excellency, Most Revd Dr Doubleday, Bishop of Brentwood.
His Excellency, Most Revd Dr Drumm, Bishop of Des Moines.
His Excellency, Most Revd Dr Dubuc, Bishop of Barquisimeto.
His Excellency, Most Revd Dr Dwyer, Bishop of Wagga-Wagga.
His Excellency, Most Revd Dr Eijo Y Garay, Bishop of Madrid.
His Excellency, Most Revd Dr Finegan, Bishop of Kilmore.
His Excellency, Most Revd Dr Fitzgerald, Bishop of Gibraltar.
His Excellency, Most Revd Dr Fitzmaurice, Bishop of Wilmington.
His Excellency, Most Revd Dr Fogarty, Bishop of Killaloe.
His Excellency, Most Revd Dr Gallagher, Bishop of Detroit.
His Excellency, Most Revd Dr Gannon, Bishop of Erie.
His Excellency, Most Revd Dr Gerlier, Bishop of Tarbes and Lourdes.
His Excellency, Most Revd Dr Gomá y Tomas, Bishop of Tarazona.
His Excellency, Most Revd Dr Gonzi, Bishop of Gozo.
His Excellency, Most Revd Dr Graham, Bishop of Tipasa.
His Excellency, Most Revd Dr Grente, Bishop of Mans.
His Excellency, Most Revd Dr Griffin, Bishop of Springfield.
His Excellency, Most Revd Dr Haggiar, Bishop of St Jean d'Acre.
His Excellency, Most Revd Dr Heelan, Bishop of Sioux City.
His Excellency, Most Revd Dr Heery, CSSp., Vicar Apostolic of S. Nigeria.
His Excellency, Most Revd Dr Heffernan, Vicar Apostolic of Zanzibar.
His Excellency, Most Revd Dr Henshaw, Bishop of Salford.
His Excellency, Right Revd Monsignor Heylen, Bishop of Namur.
His Excellency, Most Revd Dr Hoban, Bishop of Rockford.
His Excellency, Right Revd Dr Horvath, Bishop of Martyropolis.
His Excellency, Most Revd Irurita y Almándoz, Bishop of Barcelona.
His Excellency, Most Revd Dr Keane, Bishop of Limerick.
His Excellency, Right Revd Dr Keatinge, Bishop of Metellopolis.
His Excellency, Most Revd Dr Kerkhofs, Bishop of Liège.
His Excellency, Most Revd Dr Killian, Bishop of Port Augusta.
His Excellency, Most Revd Dr Kmetko, Bishop of Nitra.
His Excellency, Most Revd Dr Lafitte, Bishop of Cordoba.
His Excellency, Most Revd Dr Lee, Bishop of Clifton.
His Excellency, Most Revd Dr Le Hunsec, CSSp., Bishop of Europus.

His Excellency, Most Revd Dr Lillis, Bishop of Kansas City.
His Excellency, Most Revd Dr McCarthy, Bishop of Galloway.
His Excellency, Most Revd Dr McKenna, Bishop of Clogher.
His Excellency, Most Revd Dr McNally, Bishop of Hamilton.
His Excellency, Most Revd Dr McNamee, Bishop of Ardagh.
His Excellency, Most Revd Dr MacNeely, Bishop of Raphoe.
His Excellency, Right Revd Dr McNulty, Bishop of Nottingham.
His Excellency, Most Revd Dr MacSherry, Vicar Apostolic of Port Elizabeth.
His Excellency, Most Revd Dr Mageean, Bishop of Down and Connor.
His Excellency, Most Revd Dr Marmottin, Bishop of Saint-Dié.
His Excellency, Most Revd Dr Martin, Bishop of Argyll and The Isles.
His Excellency, Most Revd Dr Meysing, Bishop of Mina.
His Excellency, Most Revd Dr Micozzi, Bishop of Calvi et Teano.
His Excellency, Most Revd Dr de Mikes, Bishop of Szombathely.
His Excellency, Most Revd Dr Moriarty, Coadjutor Bishop of Shrewsbury.
His Excellency, Most Revd Dr Morrison, Bishop of Antigonish.
His Excellency, Most Revd Dr Morrisroe, Bishop of Achonry.
His Excellency, Most Revd Dr Mulhern, Bishop of Dromore.
His Excellency, Most Revd Dr Mulvany, Bishop of Meath.
His Excellency, Most Revd Dr Naughton, Bishop of Killala.
His Excellency, Most Revd Dr Neville, Bishop of Carrhac.
His Excellency, Most Revd Dr Nicolas, Bishop of Panopolis.
His Excellency, Most Revd Dr Norton, Bishop of Bathurst.
His Excellency, Most Revd Dr Novati, Bishop of Lodi.
His Excellency, Right Revd Dr Nuti, Bishop of Papia, Vicar Apostolic of Egypt.
His Excellency, Most Revd Dr O'Brien, Bishop of Kerry.
His Excellency, Most Revd Dr O'Doherty, Bishop of Galway.
His Excellency, Most Revd Dr O'Kane, Bishop of Derry.
His Excellency, Most Revd Dr Okoniewski, Bishop of Kulm.
His Excellency, Most Revd Dr O'Leary, OMI, Vicar Apostolic of Transvaal.
His Excellency, Most Revd Dr O'Leary, Bishop of Springfield.
His Excellency, Most Revd Dr O'Reilly, Bishop of Scranton.
His Excellency, Most Revd Dr O'Riley, Bishop of Phoba.
His Excellency, Most Revd Dr O'Rourke, Bishop of Danzig.
His Excellency, Most Revd Dr O'Rourke, Vicar Apostolic of Coast of Benin.
His Excellency, Most Revd Dr O'Sullivan, Bishop of Charlottetown.
His Excellency, Most Revd Dr Pacha, Bishop of Timisoara.
His Excellency, Most Revd Dr Pawlikowski, Bishop of Seckau.
His Excellency, Most Revd Dr Pearson, Bishop of Lancaster.
His Excellency, Most Revd Dr Pellegrino, Bishop of Bobbio.
His Excellency, Most Revd Dr Perez Platero, Bishop of Segovia.
His Excellency, Most Revd Dr Petrone, Bishop of Pozzuoli.
His Excellency, Most Revd Dr Prezdziecki, Bishop of Siedlce.
His Excellency, Most Revd Dr Provost, Bishop of Macri.

His Excellency, Most Revd Dr Rasneur, Bishop of Tournai.
His Excellency, Most Revd Dr Re, Bishop of Lipari.
His Excellency, Most Revd Dr Reinys, Bishop of Tiddi.
His Excellency, Most Revd Dr Renouf, Bishop of St George's, Newfoundland.
His Excellency, Most Revd Dr Roche, Coadjutor, Bishop of Cloyne.
His Excellency, Most Revd Dr Rodié, Bishop of Ajaccio.
His Excellency, Most Revd Dr Rohlman, Bishop of Davenport.
His Excellency, Most Revd Dr Rummell, Bishop of Omaha.
His Excellency, Most Revd Dr Ryan, Bishop of Sale.
His Excellency, Most Revd Dr Ryan, Bishop of Pembroke.
His Excellency, Most Revd Dr Schrembs, Bishop of Cleveland.
His Excellency, Most Revd Dr Shanahan, Bishop of Abila.
His Excellency, Most Revd Dr Shine, Bishop of Middlesboro.
His Excellency, Most Revd Dr Shvoy, Bishop of Székesfehérvár (Alba Reale).
His Excellency, Most Revd Dr Smit, Bishop of Paralus.
His Excellency, Most Revd Dr Staugaitis, Bishop of Telsiai.
His Excellency, Most Revd Dr Swint, Bishop of Wheeling.
His Excellency, Right Revd Dr Szelazek, Bishop of Luck.
His Excellency, Most Revd Dr Thorman, Bishop of Hexham and Newcastle.
His Excellency, Most Revd Dr Tief, Bishop of Concordia.
His Excellency, Right Revd Dr Toner, Bishop of Dunkeld.
His Excellency, Most Revd Dr Toolen, Bishop of Mobile.
His Excellency, Most Revd Dr Turner, Bishop of Buffalo.
His Excellency, Most Revd Dr Van Rechem, Bishop of Carpasia.
His Excellency, Most Revd Dr Vaughan, Bishop of Menevia.
His Excellency, Most Revd Dr Vojtassák, Bishop of Szepes.
His Excellency, Most Revd Dr Wall, Bishop of Thasos.
His Excellency, Most Revd Dr Walsh, Bishop of Charlestown.
His Excellency, Most Revd Dr Weld, Bishop of Mallstana.
His Excellency, Most Revd Dr Wilson, CSSp., Bishop of Acmonia.

Abbots:

Right Revd Dr J. Bauwens, Lord Abbot of Leffe.
Right Revd Dr H. Bennebrock, Lord Abbot of Postel.
Right Revd Dr Cabrol, Lord Abbot of Farnborough.
Right Revd Dr Golenvaux, Lord Abbot of Maredsous.
Right Revd Dr C. Guyader, Lord Abbot of Melleraie.
Right Revd Dr Hickey, O.Cist., Lord Abbot of Mount Melleray.
Right Revd Sir Hunter Blair, Lord Abbot of Dunfermline.
Right Revd Dr Knowles, Lord Abbot of Fort Augustus.
Right Revd Dr Kortschok, Lord Abbot of Reine.
Right Revd Dr Lamy, Lord Abbot of Tongerloo.
Right Revd Dr Matthews, Lord Abbot of Ampleforth.
Right Revd Dr McCarthy, Lord Abbot of Mount St Joseph's, Roscrea.

Right Revd Dr O'Connell, Lord Abbot of Mount St Bernard's, near Leicester.
Right Revd Dom Smets, Abbot General, O.Cist., Rome.
Right Revd Dr Stocker, Lord Abbot of Berne.
Right Revd Dr Strohsacker, Lord Abbot of Goettweig.
Right Revd Dr Vonier, Lord Abbot of Buckfast.
Right Revd Method Zavoral, Definitor, O.Praem., Strahow.

Superiors General:

Most Revd Dr Le Hunsec, Bishop of Europus, Superior General, CSSp.
Right Revd Dr Bernadine Balsari, Superior General, OC.
Right Revd Dr Marrani, Superior General OFM.
Right Revd P. Murray, Rector Major, CSSR.